MW01032409

THE ART AND CRAFT OF STAGE MANAGEMENT

THE ART AND CRAFT OF STAGE MANAGEMENT

DORIS SCHNEIDER
North Carolina Central University

HARCOURT BRACE COLLEGE PUBLISHERS

*Fort Worth   Philadelphia   San Diego   New York   Orlando   Austin   San Antonio
Toronto   Montreal   London   Sydney   Tokyo*

PUBLISHER	*Christopher P. Klein*
ACQUISITIONS EDITOR	*Barbara J.C. Rosenberg*
DEVELOPMENTAL EDITOR	*Cathlynn Richard*
SENIOR PROJECT EDITOR	*steve Norder*
SENIOR ART DIRECTOR	*Melinda Welch*
PRODUCTION MANAGER	*Lois West*
COVER IMAGE	*Kelly Stribling Sutherland*

Library of Congress Catalog Card Number: 96-77512

Copyright © 1997 by Harcourt Brace & Company

All rights reserved. No part of this publication may be reproduced or transmitted in any form or by any means, electronic or mechanical, including photocopy, recording, or any information storage and retrieval system, without permission in writing from the publisher.

Requests for permission to make copies of any part of the work should be mailed to: Permissions Department, Harcourt Brace & Company, 6277 Sea Harbor Drive, Orlando, Florida 32887-6777.

Address for Editorial Correspondence: Harcourt Brace College Publishers, 301 Commerce Street, Suite 3700, Forth Worth, TX 76102.

Address of Orders: Harcourt Brace & Company, 6277 Sea Harbor Drive, Orlando, FL 32887-6777. 1-800-782-4479, or 1-800-433-0001 (in Florida).

ISBN: 0-15-503023-X

Printed in the United States of America

6 7 8 9 0 1 2 3 4 5   066   10 9 8 7 6 5 4 3 2 1

DEDICATED TO THE MEMORY OF

EARL SCHNEIDER

ROLE-MODEL, FRIEND, FATHER

PREFACE

Once upon a time thirty-five years and many productions ago, a college fresh-man volunteered to work on *Arsenic and Old Lace*, the first show of the season. She was seduced not by the stage but by an attractive senior in the role of technical director. The materials for the scenery were late and crew members worked day and night for seventy-two hours, leaving only to attend classes. I lost sleep, grades, and interest in the technical director. However, the show was a success and I fell forever in love with the theatre. Of course the story did not end there. No one lives "happily ever after," but what a joyful struggle it has been. Never comfortable on stage, I became addicted to every other aspect of production. During the intervening years, I have worked as stage manager, scene designer and painter, graphics designer, costume designer, technical director, director, and always as teacher.

As an educator in a university theatre program, I often felt the greatest weakness in our production process was the lack of consistency in preparing stage managers for their role and the lack of time to prepare them adequately. This responsibility typically fell to the director, who had limited time and energy to focus in that direction. In an effort to resolve this problem without the benefit of a stage management course, I developed a set of guidelines to provide specific tasks and lend consistency to the role. In order to assure communication, organization, and clarity in notation, various production forms were designed—thus the Schneider Notation System was conceived. After fifteen years of collaborative evolution, the Notation System has been refined.

Like most colleges and universities who are recognizing the value of a trained stage manager, the university where I teach now has a course in stage management. For this course, we wanted a textbook that prepared students to stage manage within their educational environment. We wanted this experience to be as close to that of professional theatre as practical, considering the limited experience and knowledge of most first-time stage managers. To meet this need, the basic guidelines for fulfilling the role were enlarged and the Schneider Notation System, stage combat, musical productions, and theatre safety were added to create a truly unique book.

For many years only two books on stage management were widely used.

Recently, several others have emerged, which, like the early textbooks, focus on stage managing in the professional theatre. They are authored by professional stage managers and represent their personal approach to the craft. Without disputing their value, this book takes a different approach. It does not represent simply "my way of stage managing." As a teacher, I wanted to provide information from an educational as well as a professional point of view; and I wanted to present a cross-section of opinions and approaches on performing and teaching the role. In interviewing other stage managers, choreographers, fight directors, and pyrotechnists about the craft of stage management, I found that "my way" was sometimes flawed and often limited. Interviews with directors, designers, and educators, as well as stage managers, supplied different perspectives on the current state of the art of stage management.

THE PROCESS

Gerald Freedman of the North Carolina School of the Arts and Great Lakes Theatre Festival said, "**Art** is the internal need to communicate; **craft** is the skill necessary to do that." Chapter 1 introduces the **art**; the following chapters teach the **craft**. However, in studying the craft of stage management, students should be reminded to see each task as more than rote activity; they should see each task as an opportunity to evaluate and fulfill the individual needs of the production in order to make a difference in its evolution and in the final artistic product.

THE ART

Chapter 1 introduces stage management as a developing art in a highly technological profession. The role of the stage manager is examined and redefined to meet the needs of contemporary theatre.

THE PLAN

Chapter 2 provides a nuts-and-bolts plan for stage managing. It is a guide for the beginning stage manager and a review for the experienced one. Guidelines are divided into each production phase—from preproduction planning to postproduction activities. Checklists are included at the end of the chapter and can be edited to suit the production, the director, and the stage manager. As one student said of this chapter, "It takes the fear out of first-time stage managing. I know what to do and when to do it."

THE PRODUCTION BOOK

Chapter 3 discusses the format of the production book and the forms that are the heart of organization and communication. Theatrical productions (like theatre personnel) resist standardization, and do so with justification. Regardless of how well a plan or collection of forms works for one production, adjustments must be made for the next script, theatre, and director. These forms were designed with that need in mind. Instructions and samples of adapting and using the forms are included in the chapter.

BLOCKING NOTATIONS

Chapter 4 presents traditional symbols, abbreviations, and other conventions for noting the blocking of stage movement, and introduces the Schneider Notation System, which includes all of the above. Unlike the complicated dance notation systems in existence, this system is simple and easy to learn and use. The evolution of the system took fifteen years and was the result of input from stage managers and directors in both educational and professional theatres around the country. The purpose of the system is to make notating stage movement quick, accurate, and legible in an organized space.

STAGE COMBAT

Chapter 5 discusses the stage manager's responsibilities in a production that includes stage combat. It provides information on auditions, warm-ups, rehearsals, performance trouble-shooting strategies, and the care and handling of weapons. It also introduces a notation system for unarmed stage combat developed with the assistance of J. D. Martinez, director at Washington and Lee University and former president of the Society of American Fight Directors.

MUSICAL THEATRE, DANCE, AND OPERA

Chapter 6 discusses the stage manager's responsibilities within musical productions. The information parallels that of the chapter on stage combat, focusing on the particular needs of singers and dancers.

SAFETY

Chapter 7 discusses health and safety in rehearsals and performances: responsibility, the law and liability, accident prevention, emergency procedures, and first-response care.

CAREER

Chapter 8 evaluates stage management as a career choice; suggests training options; lists professional associations and publications that disseminate information and job lists; and provides guidelines for designing a resumé, building a portfolio, and preparing for an interview. This information is based on two national surveys.

APPENDIXES

The appendixes include detailed content or instructions for the stage manager's kit, technical lettering, company rules, taping the ground plan, setting up prop tables, spiking props and scenery, and numbering and calling cues.

This book addresses the beginning stage manager specifically. However, because of the growing responsibilities of stage managers in the contemporary theatre, much of the information is valuable even to experienced stage managers. The text provides guidelines for:

1. Beginning stage managers
2. Experienced stage managers who want to augment their knowledge and evaluate alternative approaches to notating blocking of stage movement, unarmed combat, and dance
3. Directors who want to encourage maximum input from this central member of their production staff in order to be freed of administrative concerns, who want the benefits of a nurtured and protected collaboration with the other visual and performing artists, and who want to be assured of a maintenance of the interpretation and evolved concepts
4. Teachers who want to prepare drama students to creatively and efficiently carry out their roles as stage managers rather than perpetuating the frustrating and unproductive method of trial-and-error.

ACKNOWLEDGMENTS

The following people represent the major contributors to the textbook and persons interviewed for additional information and opinions on the art and craft of stage management: Johnny Alston, departmental chair and technical director at North Carolina Central University; Dayna Anderson, professor of stage management at Schuford School of Drama, Catawba College; William C. Brown, freelance stage manager and lighting designer; Carol Clark, freelance AEA stage manager; Thomas Connell, AGMA, production stage manager at the Metropolitan Opera House; Diane Crews, freelance director, playwright, and educator; Rick Cunningham, head of stage management training at the Professional Theatre Training School, University of Delaware; Brandon Daughtry, freelance director and playwright; Susan Evanston, SAFD, Northern Kentucky University; Vincent Foote, professor, School of Design at North Carolina State University; Eric Forsythe, head of stage management, acting, and directing at the University of Iowa; Drew Fracher, SAFD fight choreographer; Gerald Freedman, North Carolina School of the Arts and Great Lakes Theatre Festival; Elizabeth Grimes, freelance stage manager, technical director, and arts educator; Christopher Jones, associate professor of theatre arts at Northern Illinois University; Linda Kerr-Norflett, director at North Carolina Central University; Barry Kornhauser, AEA stage manager and playwright in residence at the Fulton Opera House; Ming Cho Lee, professor at Yale School of Drama and a scene designer; Wenghai Ma, scene designer at Duke University; J. D. Martinez, director and fight choreographer at Washington and Lee University; Evelyn Matten, AEA stage manager at the American Players Theatre; Marie Merkel, freelance production stage manager for opera; Lloyd Richards, director at the Eugene O'Neill Theatre; Kimberly Strange, freelance AEA stage manager; Richard Sillen, pyrotechnician at Actors' Theatre of Louisville; Wesley Van Tassel, Central Washington University; Randolph Umberger, director and playwright at North Carolina Central University; and Craig Weindling, freelance AEA stage manager.

In addition, a special gratitude should go to the following people for their tireless assistance and contributions: Dayna Anderson, William C. Brown, Rick Cunningham, Brandon Daughtry, Wenhai Ma, J. D. Martinez, and the editorial and production staff at Harcourt Brace College Publishers, including the art director, Melinda Welch; the production manager, Lois West; and particularly the project editor, steve Norder, a respecter and protector of books. Many thanks to all the participants at various conferences, professional associations, and universities, who took the Schneider Notation System and tossed it around, stepped on it, uplifted it, uplifted it, tried it out, and ultimately gave it shape and form.

Doris Schneider
June 1996

NOTE TO STUDENTS

My first role as stage manager was assigned to me by Obra L. Quave, who was also my first director and later my first teaching colleague. When he read his company rules to the cast, he always began with, "Thou shalt respect the stage manager." I think his second rule was, "Thou shalt take a shower before rehearsals." There were many other rules, but these stick in my memory and still serve me well. He did not, of course, mean that they should respect the person but rather the role of stage manager. Each of us had to earn personal respect by the way we played our role. This is your challenge.

DS

CONTENTS

THE ART AND CRAFT OF STAGE MANAGEMENT

THE ART OF STAGE MANAGEMENT

THE ART

The purpose of this textbook is to introduce you to the world of stage management. Managing the performance stage has evolved from the ranks of unskilled labor to become a distinguished craft and is now regarded by many as an art form. Clearly, all three levels of stage management–labor, craft, and art–continue to coexist in the theater, being dependent as they are on the experience, sensitivity, creativity, and professionalism of the individual stage manager and the environment in which the manager is encouraged to develop and contribute artistically.

In this way, stage management is no different than playwrighting, directing, designing, and acting: Each profession includes hacks, craftspersons, and artists. In each can be found practitioners who are pushed or held back by the leadership and expectations which allow or restrict creativity and individual expression.

The role of stage manager has historically required general theatre knowledge and a disciplined, organized, nurturing spirit. These are still prerequisites. However, the modern production is developing in a direction that demands much more of this living conduit between the various components of a theatrical production.

In the last several decades, a tremendous growth in the technological advancements of productions as well as a movement towards specialization have parented compartmentalization. *This process, in which distinct production areas work independently for the majority of the rehearsal process and come together for a comparatively short time during tech week, has fostered the need for stage managers who can participate in*

*as well as facilitate the collaboration process. The stage manager must
also have the sensitivity and knowledge to call these technologically
complex shows with the timing and control necessary to communicate
and maintain the director's concept.*

—RICK CUNNINGHAM, UNIVERSITY OF DELAWARE

In facilitating collaboration between all of the production artists as well as
organizing and running rehearsals and performances, a myriad of organizational tasks must be accomplished by the stage manager. Any novice may be
able to complete a list of assigned tasks. Through successful and repeated experience, the novice even may achieve the label of craftsman. Only when the
list is flexible and is secondary to collaboration, perception, anticipation, and
sensitive problem solving is the stage manager approaching the art. When the
willingness to take risks and contribute through creative exposure and participation leads to a more unified and richer performance, the stage manager is
practicing the art. Though the artistry of the stage manager is, by its own nature, less obvious than that of the designer and director, it is equally important
in the final success of the performance, and in the maintenance of the production family, it is perhaps even more important.

Look again at those common terms that describe and define the qualities
separating the hack from the artist.

Collaboration and its facilitation is one of the stage manager's primary
responsibilities. It is the heart of the theatrical production.

Collaboration is a process performed by artists sharing their individual
knowledge, experience, and responses in a guided atmosphere of trust,
flexibility, and openness, fostering the evolution of a new and unified entity:
an idea, an emotion, or a vision.

The stage manager is the guardian of the process, encouraging participation,
clarifying misunderstandings, and protecting creative exposure.

Perception means making full use of one's senses (including intuition) to
identify potential needs, conflicts, and dangers for individuals as well as the
overall production.

Anticipation means to fulfill needs before being asked to do so, to address
potential conflicts or growing disharmony before they become major issues, and
to eliminate dangerous or hazardous conditions before someone is hurt.

Sensitive problem solving first and foremost means diplomacy. It also implies
creativity and sometimes discretion and kindness in looking for the best
solution—not just a solution.

Participation, in this instance, means participating in the creative aspects of the
production.

The most enjoyable experience of my career took place at the Actor's Theatre of Louisville under the direction of Tina Landau. I was involved in the creative collaboration for an ensemble development piece called 1969.

—CRAIG WEINDLING, AEA STAGE MANAGER

Our higher education system is challenged to prepare stage managers who can be looked to not only for management but also for input. After all, if they do not analyze and conceptualize, how can they respond to and maintain the concepts of others? In this increasingly more mechanized and specialized society and profession, each participant in the theatrical process must be encouraged to use creative resources, make judgements, and take risks rather than slavishly follow a list of tasks.

Treating the stage manager as merely a craftsperson *can cause the development of a cynical, noncreative attitude, thereby limiting that stage manager's contributions.*

—ERIC FORSYTHE, UNIVERSITY OF IOWA

Student stage managers must be treated as creative artists even at the lowest level. Otherwise, they will not feel fully engaged in the process.

—CHRIS JONES, NORTHERN ILLINOIS UNIVERSITY

There is an art to stage management. However, fulfilling the art includes knowing and meeting or surpassing the standards of the profession and doing so with conscious ethical behavior.

Professionalism is not based on salary or union membership. Artistry is not professionalism, and conversely, professionalism is not artistry; but the two certainly complement each other. Professionalism implies high quality labor as well as preparation, organization, and discipline. Professionalism enhances the art and the craft.

A professional is recognized by attitude and quality of work, by a knowledge of the standards of the profession, and by the ability to apply those standards—even in nonprofessional circumstances.

—ERIC FORSYTHE, UNIVERSITY OF IOWA

Stage managers are in a tricky position, poised between management and artists, and responsible to both. How they handle themselves in that position becomes the measure of their professionalism.

—LLOYD RICHARDS, EUGENE O'NEILL THEATRE

Ethical behavior in any profession implies honesty, loyalty, fairness, and decency, both in personal behavior within the profession and in the treatment of colleagues.

*A stage manager must protect the integrity of the process and the art form
and ensure that everyone is treated like a decent human being. In theatre,
there are many opportunities for ethical lapses. This can range from unfair
treatment of one actor over another to pay checks that bounce.*

—CHRIS JONES, NORTHERN ILLINOIS UNIVERSITY

When an actor or member of the artistic staff becomes vulnerable in order to be
creatively expressive, ethics demands that this vulnerability be protected in order
that it may be productive. The stage manager is in a position to empower the
creativity of an individual, to maintain rather than undermine the production
family by discouraging negativity, to anticipate and eliminate (rather than overlook)
health and safety hazards, and to facilitate and contribute to collaboration. Good
ethical behavior will not make a stage manager artistic, but it is an important
quality in the art of the profession.

Family refers to the production company. The long hours of working in an
atmosphere where exploration and exposure of emotional as well as creative
depths and limitations requires a cooperative and supportive spirit. The stage
manager's maintenance of this spirit of family is as important to the quality of the
production as a talented cast or a strong artistic staff.

Calling the show is the stage manager's performance. The success of this
performance is measured by the stage manager's ability to maintain the
director's concept of rhythm, timing, intensity, and flow. Because the actors are
live before a live audience, their timing and interpretation can vary from one
performance to the next. Therefore, the cueing of the actors and technicians is
not mechanical. It must be continually adjusted to fit the unexpected. In a
technically complex show, the cueing is the pulse of the production.

THE ROLE

Stage management has been a viable career option for years. However, there
is still a lack of definition for the role in the nonprofessional theatre. The skills
and tasks required can be limited to those of a "gopher" or enlarged to include
complete responsibility for running and maintaining rehearsals and performances, both onstage and backstage. Actors Equity Association (AEA or
Equity) publishes a handbook which specifies the duties and obligations of a
card-carrying union stage manager. All stage managers should be familiar
with the AEA Handbook, whether they are union or not. However, for every
Equity stage manager, there are dozens of beginning and developing stage
managers in university, community, and nonunion regional theatres who
must define their jobs anew with each production, producer, and director.
Sometimes circumstances necessitate challenging archaic company traditions
in order to gain the respect and responsibilities currently associated with the

title. For these individuals in particular, this textbook provides guidelines for properly determining and tactfully carrying out each aspect of the stage manager's role.

Even in nonprofessional theatre, a stage manager will rarely work alone. Modern production demands require an expanded staff. Delegation of tasks to this staff will vary according to experience and production needs. Care should be taken to assign proper titles to each role, thus avoiding confusion and duplication in responsibility. The following titles and job descriptions are standard in educational as well as professional theatre.

The **stage manager** (SM) is responsible for running rehearsals and performances. In addition, the SM leads production meetings and maintains a chain of communication between the theatre staff and artists, builds and maintains the production book, notes and corrects all blocking during rehearsals, and calls all cues from the control booth during technical rehearsals and performances. After the show has opened, the SM is charged with maintaining the integrity of the director's interpretation of the script, maintaining the physical elements of the production (scenery, costumes, etc.), and maintaining the cast and crews as "family."

The **assistant stage manager** (ASM) is a distinct position with its own accountabilities. The word "assistant" is a misnomer. The ASM is assigned specific tasks to aid in the smooth running of rehearsals and performances, which may range from rehearsing dance or stage combat, to giving line cues and running props, to total responsibility backstage during technical rehearsals and performances. If the stage manager calls cues from the control booth, an ASM on each side of the stage is desirable. In a musical production or a heavy scenery and/or prop show, it is common to have two or more ASMs.

The **production assistant** (PA) is responsible to the ASM and may be given tasks such as supervising stage crews, calling line cues, sweeping the stage, and so on. There may be more than one PA, depending on the size and complexity of the show.

The **production stage manager** (PSM) is a loosely used title. Sometimes this title is assigned to the producer's assistant who acts as a trouble-shooter for the producer; it also may be a permanent staff position for a company or educational theatre program which involves coordination of rehearsal time and space for multiple productions and supervision and/or training of all SMs working in that theatre; it may be assigned to an SM responsible for several productions being performed simultaneously (such as an evening of one-acts, each having its own SM); or it may be given to an SM gratuitously, as a program credit, with no changes in responsibilities.

QUALIFICATIONS

The qualifications for stage managers vary according to the company or theatre recruiting for the position. Many community as well as educational theatres have no experienced stage managers within their pool of talent and may therefore have to assign the role to an unsuspecting novice who, hopefully, has organizational, communication, and "people" skills. In addition, she/he should be able to lead as well as follow, handle chains of command, think independently and creatively, arbitrate, diffuse stress, and be willing to commit an abundance of time and energy to the production. These are the basic personality requirements. The practical tasks of the job can be learned.

ARE YOU READY TO BEGIN?

The information in this text can guide you through a production experience, but a student of the art of stage management should seek a broad knowledge of and experience in all aspects of theatre and the performing arts in general. This knowledge and experience will promote an understanding and respect for the rest of the production team and will enhance communication and the manager's ability to collaborate. However, this is an ongoing growth process and the lack of experience should not prevent or postpone your first assignment as stage manager.

In the past, stage managers (even for the professional theatre) competed for jobs with out-of-work actors, would-be directors, or someone's secretary, girlfriend, or relative. The attitude often was "anyone can stage manage." There were no specific skills required, although it helped if you could make good coffee and did not expect pay. "Stage management can't be taught" or "stage managers are born, not made" were the next attitudes held by those who believed the role required a nurturing personality and common sense. These qualities help but are not enough to fulfill the emerging role of stage manager which is one of the most stressful roles in an already high-stress profession. Preparation and organization (the core of this text), augmented by experience and a general knowledge of theatre crafts will aid you in reducing this stress and assist you in maintaining order, calm, and efficiency. Although the role of stage manager has gained the respect and appreciation it deserves, it is not a job for someone who needs continual acknowledgment. Your reward is witnessing a production which is better than it could have been without you, because of your contributions through the art of stage management.

THE CRAFT:
NUTS AND BOLTS

2

Stage managing is the perfect example of catch-22: You have to be sane to carry out the job; you have to be insane to want the job. You cannot get membership in the Actors' Equity Association (AEA) without a professional contract; you cannot get a professional contract without membership in Equity. If a performance is technically perfect, others will be praised; if a performance is technically flawed, you will be blamed. You are not considered a member of the artistic staff, the technical staff, or the management staff; but you work with all three. Yours is a position of authority but you will have to sweep the floor. In fact, the range and number of tasks associated with your job is staggering. Stage management can be the toughest role in theatre today. However, there is a resolution for every contradiction, even for getting your Equity card.

This chapter will assist you in bringing stability to an inherently unstable profession through *preparation, communication, organization,* and *anticipation.* The following pages outline a nuts-and-bolts approach to the craft of stage management, allowing you to construct an individualized plan for each division of the rehearsal and performance process. However, remember that no plan is foolproof or is appropriate for every production. Each theatre company has its own particular mission, its own hierarchy, its own specific practices and rules. Therefore, any plan must remain flexible enough to adapt to the special needs of the company as well as the physical theatre, the script, the schedule, and your own personal style.

The beginning stage manager must focus on craft until it is second nature and then move on to the next level. Craft is not demeaning.

—CAROL CLARK, AEA STAGE MANAGER

The terms "craft" and "craftsman(woman)" definitely are not demeaning: They imply skill and the ability to create a product of high quality and value.

PREPARATION

Do as much ground work as you can prior to auditions and rehearsals. Evaluate the company, the theatre, and your own role in the production. Who is in charge? Who answers to whom? Who does what? Who will be your immediate superior? To whom do you go with information, problems, reports, and requests? The power structure and role assignments will vary based on the type of theatre and the size of the staff. (See Figure 2-1 for a typical organizational chart.)

> The **producer,** usually at the top of the power structure, is in charge of the business of the theatre. In professional theatre, the producer is an individual representing the investors; in community theatre, the producer may be an individual or a committee representing the membership; and in most educational theatres, the academic department is the producer representing the institution.

> The **production manager** has responsibilities which can vary from one company to another, and in many companies, the role may not exist. Usually a liaison to management, the production manager is above the stage manager in company hierarchy but does not supervise or problem-solve for the SM.

> The **director** is responsible for interpreting the script, collaborating with the designers in order to maintain visual unity, blocking and refining the actors' interpretations, and coordinating the various artistic aspects of the production.

> The **stage manager** answers to both the producer and director and assumes as many of the director's management tasks as possible in order to free the director to direct.

> The **designers** collaborate with the director on visual concepts and artistic decisions. They provide renderings which the technical director and the crews bring to life.

> The **technical director** is usually responsible for most technical aspects of a production such as scenery, lighting, sound, and those crews.

In a small company with a limited staff, one person may be assigned many roles. For example, the technical director may be responsible for all technical aspects of a production: designing, building, and painting scenery; designing and hanging lights; designing, recording, and creating sound; and running technical rehearsals. In a company with a larger staff, the technical director may only build the scenery and supervise technical crews during technical rehearsals. Figure 2-1 represents a typical organization of personnel for a musical production. Remember that it will vary from one theatre and one production to another.

If you are new to the company, meet and establish a working rapport with each staff member. If you have an understanding of their jobs and the restrictions and latitudes surrounding their work, you will be better able to interface with them when the time comes for you to do so.

FIGURE 2.1

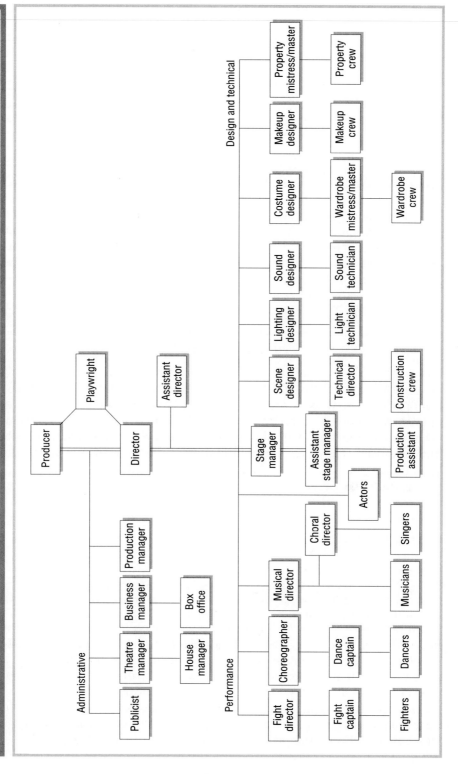

COMMUNICATION

Determine your responsibilities as stage manager and establish lines of communication. Be sure both you and your supervisor understand what is expected of you, and if you are being paid, get those expectations in writing, preferably in the form of a contract, before work begins. An undefined job description may grow to unrealistic proportions if a paycheck is held over your head. If you are an Equity union member, your job description and salary are within specified union guidelines. Otherwise, you must negotiate for yourself.

One of the stage manager's most important tasks is communicating and collaborating effectively with the director. The stage manager is the director's right hand throughout the production process. However, in educational and community theatre, some directors will not be accustomed to efficient stage management or to working with a stage manager at all, while other directors are very specific about what they want and need from the SM. Meet with the director to discuss your responsibilities.

ORGANIZATION

A checklist (an organized listing of tasks and responsibilities) for stage managers is not a new idea. Many companies have their own. The checklists in this chapter provide guidelines for SM tasks in a typical theatre production. That means they probably will need to be reviewed and adapted each time they are used. They are a ground plan for communicating with the director about your contributions to the production. Some directors will choose to retain certain tasks as their own, while others will add duties to the stage manager's checklists. However, good organization is meaningless if it ends with paperwork. See each task through to completion and be conscientious about the manner in which it is carried out.

ANTICIPATION AND EXPECTATION

The checklists of SM tasks are not contracts which limit your contributions to a production. Meeting minimal requirements is just that—minimal. Anticipate rehearsal and performance needs that you or one of your staff can fill; anticipate unsafe situations for actors or crews and see that they are corrected; anticipate conflicts and try to resolve them before they become obstacles to a smooth production. Expect of yourself, as well as the rest of the company, commitment to the project, discipline, respect and appreciation for each person's contributions, and professionalism.

Although you are in a position of authority, resist becoming a dictator. In order for your cast to respond quickly during stressful rehearsals or performances, they must respect you and your role as stage manager. Your own standards of behavior will influence everyone's:

1. Use traditional theatre etiquette. Say "please" and "thank you" when asking for responses from the cast and crew. Ask them to do the same. Choice of words and the manner in which they are said often take the sting out of an unpleasant task or a criticism.

2. You are the liaison between the director and the cast as well as other members of the staff. Individuals may not agree with the director's interpretation or directorial style. Address problems rather than encourage them and never participate in gossip. It can undermine the production and divide the production family. There are differing opinions as to where the stage manager's loyalty should be focused: on the director, the actors, or the production. All three must always be considered and each situation individually addressed.

    The stage manager's responsibility as a creative artist is to act with sensitivity rather than take the safe road at the production's expense. For example, I worked with a famous director who missed a lot. The actors knew it and came to me for advice. I had to talk to the director in a way that did not threaten his authority. It ultimately became a good production. And I got a lot of work because I took a risk.

    —ERIC FORSYTHE, UNIVERSITY OF IOWA

3. Use ethical behavior in working with each artist who must emotionally or intellectually expose him/herself in order to respond to the script and participate in the collaborative process.

4. Actors are (by necessity) sensitive. They often have very high "highs" and very low "lows" and can leap from one to the other in the space of a breath. Get to know your cast well enough to individually encourage them to be their productive best, but beware of becoming everyone's pal. It is difficult to criticize or fine someone who thinks of you as a best friend. Some professional distance will be necessary for the **run** of the show.

5. Use proper channels and diplomacy.

    Allow things to go through proper channels. You are involved in a lot of privileged information and must know what you can talk about.

    —CAROL CLARK, AEA STAGE MANAGER

    I learned an important lesson in diplomacy early in my stage-management career. A director commented in confidence that a prop looked obscene. I jokingly passed the comment on and the designer (who had not intended obscenity) threatened to leave the production.

—ERIC FORSYTHE, UNIVERSITY OF IOWA

6. The way in which you disseminate information (which can include orders and/or criticisms), can make the difference between a person feeling confident and empowered or insecure and degraded. Your manner will affect the whole emotional climate of rehearsals and performances.

You are responsible for the smooth running of auditions, rehearsals, production meetings, and performances. You do not have to do everything yourself, but you should make sure that everything gets done by someone. "That's not my job" or "I assumed someone else would do it" are poor excuses for a slowed rehearsal or a flawed performance. The more efficiently you do your job, the more time and energy the director will have for refining the production.

This is not a step-by-step recipe book just as a theatrical production is not a combination of measured ingredients mixed or layered for public consumption. Each performance in the living theatre is a one-of-a-kind piece of three-dimensional art which evolves as it is produced. The ingredients must remain flexible. In other words, keep an aesthetic eye open, keep an eraser handy, keep your back to the wall, and stay loose.

PREPRODUCTION

You will never have as much time to get things done as you have before the first rehearsals. Once they begin, you will be amazed at how your time is consumed with projects born from rehearsals. Do not waste this valuable preparation time. Use the *checklist* (p. 70) to keep your daily goals organized. If your production requires forms not provided in this text, create new ones.

Many tasks in this chapter refer you to props people, costume people, management staff, and so on. In some companies these positions may not exist or the personnel may not be available until after rehearsals begin. In their absence, do the tasks yourself or have someone on your staff do them. You are responsible for getting things done—not for doing them all yourself. Because a verbal request can easily be forgotten or denied, always document work assignments and keep a copy of any memos that verify tasks or requested deadlines.

Make a copy of the *preproduction checklist* (p. 43) and of all the forms in Chapter 3 that are appropriate to your production. They may be enlarged on an office copier at 142 percent of their existing size in order to fill out an 8 1/2-by-11-inch format. (A greater percentage could be used depending upon individual copying machines.) Using the instructions in Chapter 3, edit the checklist and forms to suit the director, the production, and yourself.

1. Make working copies of the forms. If you do not have access to a copy machine, assign this task to someone who does. Be sure you or your helper learns how to use the machine properly and can locate the copy supplies.

2. Order scripts (if this has not already been done). Consult with the director for the number needed. Sometimes a director will cut roles, add parts, or use **understudies.** A script can be divided for minor characters who are not on stage simultaneously.

3. Read the script first for an emotional and intellectual response. You can talk about concept better if you have one yourself. Read it a second time to evaluate it for problems such as a large cast, multiple sets, **quick changes,** and so on.

4. Number the scripts and maintain the *script record* (p. 71). Scripts are sometimes made available for actors to borrow and read before auditions. Give a before-auditions deadline for their return.

5. Ask for an information packet on the performance space. This usually includes a ground plan, lists of curtains, lighting equipment, sound equipment, electronic communication system, and so on. If there is no packet for that space, visit it and fill out the *theatre information* sheets (pp. 72 & 73). Take an assistant and a tape measure. Ask someone who knows the space to show you around and help you locate **work lights,** fuse boxes, fire extinguishers, and so on.

6. Meet with the director to discuss the production. Get information on style, interpretation, period, and so on. Reading the script will not necessarily provide you with this information.

> *I spent a summer researching the Greek classical theatre in preparation for designing* Antigone. *Imagine my surprise when the director told me the play was to be set in contemporary Africa.*
>
> —DORIS SCHNEIDER

A good director has something personal and possibly unpredictable to add to the interpretation of a production. Do not judge his or her choices. What seems irrational or even bizarre in early discussions may become very logical and insightful in performance. Take notes at every meeting. Never assume that you will remember anything. Use the *production fact sheet* (p. 74) to collect additional information on the script and company.

> *NOTE: To assure clarity on all written communication, it is recommended that you type or hand letter using standard technical lettering. See Appendix B for guidelines and worksheets.*

7. Determine the size of the SM staff needed for this production. If the staff is not complete, get permission to recruit the remaining personnel. Meet with the SM staff and assign duties. Using the checklists as a guide, delegate these duties evenly and appropriately. Document assignments so there is no confusion or denial later on. Discuss the production and your expectations of each member of your staff. If there are first-timers, discuss the role of stage manager in general and for this theatre company in particular. Make everyone aware of the time commitment involved and identify any schedule conflicts.

8. Schedule a time and place for the first production meeting and notify the staff. Subsequent meetings may not require the full staff, but every staff member available should attend the first one.

If you know the theatre and its politics, you may be in a position to run the meeting. If you are new, you may spend the first meeting learning as much about the company as the production. If there is a production manager, he/she may run the meetings. As a regional theatre stage manager, I've been in both situations an equal number of times.

—CRAIG WEINDLING, AEA STAGE MANAGER

Prepare a meeting place with tables and/or an adequate number of desks. Prepare an agenda with input from the director. Your primary responsibilities in running the production meetings are to make sure everyone gets an opportunity for input and communication is clear and complete (no one leaves the meeting with the wrong idea); and to anticipate and resolve misunderstandings or personality conflicts (no one leaves the meeting wanting to resign).

Problems between the artistic staff can surface outside of production meetings where they are normally addressed and solved. If not recognized early, they can steam-roll to proportions which can affect the quality of the production.

—ERIC FORSYTHE, UNIVERSITY OF IOWA

9. In the first production meeting, do the following:

   ■ Using the *production meeting* form (p. 75), take voluminous notes.
   ■ Collect information for the production calendar. Watch for conflicts with other productions, holidays, and so on. Add deadlines for building estimated time of arrival (ETAs) from the technical director, the props master/mistress, and the costumer. If the company allows them, get cutoff dates (time after which nothing new can be requested) from props and costumes. Add the publicity schedule (including photo shoots) from the publicist. Inform all staff of shoot dates as far in advance as possible in case certain **props** and costumes need to be pulled

or built by those dates. Add dates for the **dress parade** and **technical rehearsals** and for any additional information needed for the production calendar.

- Consult with the director, **choreographer, fight director,** and **costume designer** about rehearsal costumes and props. Any costume pieces, which actors must learn to move in comfortably and safely, should be introduced early in rehearsals.

- Discuss music and **sound effects** and schedule their integration into rehearsals.

- Discuss special lighting, which may affect safety or actor orientation, and schedule its integration into rehearsals.

- Discuss any **special effects** such as fog or pyrotechnics, which need to be assigned to specialists or taught to an ASM or a member of the **running crew.**

- Ask for correct spelling of staff and personnel names and titles for the program. Use the *program information approval* form (p. 76). If crews are already set, add their names to the form.

- Set a date and time for the next production meeting.

10. Plan how the **auditions** will be run. Each director has a preference. For example, the actors may watch each other audition, or they may be brought in one or two at a time. They may be asked to present prepared monologues, **cold readings, improvisations,** and so on.

    Communicate with the director, music director, choreographer, and fight director about particular needs for auditions such as props, piano, temporary dance floor, weapons, protective padding, mats, and so on. Request their delivery to the audition site at the appropriate time.

11. Get approval of the *audition* form (p. 78). The director may ask you to edit the audition form to suit the play and the preferred audition process. Make more copies of audition forms than you anticipate needing because the number of performers who will audition is difficult to predict.

12. Plan the text for the audition notices. Minimal information would include date, time, place, preparation required (if any), and the name of the producing company. Additional information might include number and types of roles available, special skills needed (such as singing, dancing, fencing, tumbling, etc.), appropriate clothing, play title and playwright, publisher version (if a classic), production dates, and portfolio requirements (all professional theatre companies and some community and educational companies require a resumé and photograph). Across-the-board special requirements (such as haircuts, hair coloring, nudity, etc.) should also be included on the audition notice. If these criteria for a role affect only one or two actors, the information may be included in a paragraph on the audition information sheet.

Type the information or give the text copy to the publicist for preparation for printing. It may be professionally printed or copied on an office machine. Post the audition notices.

13. Acquire keys to all spaces to which you need access. Be sure there are duplicates to all keys you are given, and if you lose them, notify the appropriate staff person immediately.

14. Reserve the audition site. One room is needed for actors to fill out forms and wait to be called and another for the actual auditions. If the production includes music, dance, or combat, you may identify several additional rooms for auditions as well as one for warming up. If these room(s) are used for other activities between auditions and call-backs, locate a lockable space for any equipment or props.

15. Post an audition notice and any additional audition information or instructions on the **callboard** (bulletin board reserved for all communication

A notice for open auditions is posted on a callboard. The callboard is cleared of everything else except the production title to draw attention to the flyer. (Photo by J. B. Alston)

concerning the production). For example, if it is an original or lesser known script, you might post a summary of the plot and a description of the characters. Also post a sheet explaining the audition procedure and listing the rooms being used for waiting, warming up, and auditioning.

Inspect the audition site and be sure there are adequate desks, tables, chairs, and so on. If the space needs cleaning, have it done. If the space is too cold or too hot, get instructions and permission for adjusting the temperature as needed. Dancers need warmer spaces than actors do for warming up and auditioning.

16. Locate and evaluate the contents of the stage manager's kit. This box/bag/ case holds supplies and equipment to promote the smooth running of auditions, rehearsals, and performances. It includes everything from cough drops and ice packs to extra fuses and batteries. Accidents and emergencies can occur in auditions just as they can in rehearsals. A sample list of contents is provided in Appendix A. Use petty cash to maintain the kit.

17. Request petty cash from the business manager. Ask for the preferred record-keeping procedure. Document expenditures and always save receipts. Label each receipt with your initials and the department (props, costumes, etc.) for which the purchase was made.

If you are assigned to schedule activities that involve personnel who are paid by the hour, request information on budget allocations. Proper scheduling, correct management of fragile props and costumes, and strict control over care and handling of backstage equipment and supplies can help the company meet its budget.

18. Paperwork is one of your most time-consuming tasks. A desk with drawers or file space is necessary for carrying out and maintaining this work. Office space is also desirable but not always accessible. Ask about sharing an office in order to have a quiet place to write and a lockable place for keeping your materials. One solution is to be creative—turn a dressing room or a storage room or other "found" space into a temporary office.

AUDITIONS

Your primary responsibilities in auditions are:

- to make the procedure run as smoothly as possible
- to assist the director in any way you can

The best way to assure the former is to have the procedure explained thoroughly on paper and posted on the callboard and to make appropriate use of your staff. To assure the latter, assign yourself or an **ASM** to sit with the director and document each audition. Continue to anticipate additional needs.

Make a copy of the *audition checklist* (p. 44), edit it to suit your production needs, and use it as a guide.

Be patient in answering questions and calming nervous performers and tense staff. Your confidence and assurance can ease tensions and allow their creative spirits to function.

1. Be early for auditions so that the space can be set up and ready for the process to begin at the time scheduled. Post signs leading actors to the appropriate rooms to warm up or to wait to be called.

2. Use your staff to manage the flow of people. For example, one person may hand out audition forms and pencils, answer questions, and assist auditionees. Another person might receive the completed paperwork and take it to the audition space. Using these forms, list each performer on the *audition notes/schedule* form (p. 80). Assign your staff in whatever way best suits the situation so that you are free to assist the director.

    If the play has music, there may be simultaneous auditions for actors, dancers, singers, and musicians. You may need to recruit production assistants (PAs) to assist with the flow of people and you may need to supervise this, assigning an ASM to sit with the director. See Chapters 5 & 6 for additional information on combat and dance auditions.

Geoff Zeger auditions for a role in *I'm Not Rappaport* to be presented at North Carolina Central University. Zeger is provided with a chair and a spotlighted area for his audition. (Photo by J. B. Alston)

3. If auditions are held **onstage** and under stage lights, mark (with tape or chalk) the place where the actor can be seen best.

4. During auditions, you or an ASM will take notes for the director. Keep a list of who read what with whom and note identifying physical characteristics or clothing (such as "military hair cut" or "red sweater") to aid in remembering the auditionee later. Maintain paperwork. Be sure audition forms have all contact information (phone number and address), local as well as permanent. Time audition pieces if there is a time limit. Call actors in to read. Read with actors if asked. Do not try to draw focus to yourself, but read with some feeling so the auditionee will have something to which he/she may respond.

5. After auditions, secure props and return the room to its original setup.

6. After the director selects the performers for callbacks (those who will audition a second time), type the list. Include on this list the date, time, and place for callback auditions and post it on the callboard. Provide the company secretary with a copy of the callback list so that people who phone for audition results can be saved a trip to the theatre. The company policy may be to telephone each auditionee with the information.

7. Run callbacks the same as auditions. This phase of the auditions is often less formal. The director may combine performers in groups rather than seeing them one or two at a time.

8. After callback auditions, the director will select the final **cast.** Type the names on a *cast list* form (p. 81) and post it. If necessary, phone each person on the list. Beside the cast list, post the following: a thank-you note to everyone who auditioned; instructions to initial the cast list as acceptance of the role; time and place of the first **read-through;** the location of the production callboard (if different); a posting time and instructions for the cast to *check the callboard every day.*

9. Using the script record, assign scripts to each cast member and make them available through a central office so that actors may read the play before the first rehearsal. Get scripts to each staff member who does not already have one.

PREREHEARSAL

Even though there may be very little time between auditions and the first rehearsals, some planning simply cannot be done until after the cast is selected. Each cast member's individual skill, experience, and even physical size will influence many decisions. For example, if you have a character who must leap over a fence and your actor is not athletic, this may affect the height of the fence; if you have a **chorus** with little dance experience, you may need to

Corrugated backing provides color and allows for easy use of tacks or push pins on this sample callboard. The board is neatly organized and free of extraneous (non-production) information. The rehearsal schedule (center) is enlarged from six weeks to nine weeks. (Photo by J. B. Alston)

schedule additional time for dance rehearsals; if you have a church choir positioned on a raised platform and most of them are large, this may affect position, dimensions, and structure of the platform as well as color and design of the costumes. To ensure a good start, schedule the first production meeting with the entire staff as early as possible after the cast is set.

Meet with the director to establish rehearsal preferences and procedures.

Make a copy of the *prerehearsal checklist* (p. 45), adapt it to your production needs, and use it as a guide.

1.   Set up the callboard. One board or one designated space on the callboard should be reserved for information on your production. You can decorate this space to make it easily identified with the production. If the callboard is large enough, section it for cast, crews, and staff. Keep it current, always removing dated information; keep it neat and orderly so that information can be easily seen and read; and date all posted materials.

2.   The *calendar six weeks* form (p. 82) can be used for scheduling rehearsals and performances of the production. The number of weeks required to rehearse a production vary with the demands of the production and with the type of company. Create an appropriate calendar. Post pertinent information about the show: title, playwright, staff, cast, production dates, and so on. Attach a folder to the callboard and fill it with schedule forms (*calendar week* form, p. 83). Post directions for actors to complete the form and a deadline for its return. It can also be used to organize your own daily activities.

3.   Ask the staff and personnel to complete schedule forms.

4.   After all schedules have been returned, fill out a *contact sheet* (p. 84). Make copies of the completed form and distribute them to each member of the production staff. As the production develops, new staff and cast may be added to the list and people may change phone numbers and addresses. Keep this form (above all other forms) updated and accurate.

5.   Select the rehearsal space, keeping in mind the appropriate type of floor if dance is involved (see Chapter 6). Additional considerations might include access to a telephone, a copy machine, drinking water, and restrooms.

6.   Meet with the building supervisor in which your rehearsal space is housed to locate fuse boxes, thermostat, fire escapes, and so on. If the theatre is your rehearsal space, meet with the technical director. Ask for a copy of local fire, police, and municipal regulations. If firearms are to be used, ask for these regulations or contact the local fire marshall and obtain them for yourself. Look for potential dangers or problems such as leaks, loose floor boards, and so on. Arrange for appropriate rehearsal lights and locate replacement lamps (bulbs). Get a broom, dustpan, mop, and trashcans. Safety is one of your top priorities. Use this meeting to learn everything you need to know to establish and maintain a safe rehearsal environment.

7.   Meet with the director to discuss the rehearsal schedule, and his/her preferred procedure. Make a list of the questions you need answered. For example,

   - Are rehearsals open or closed to visitors?
   - Is smoking allowed?
   - How many, when, and for how long should breaks be scheduled?
   - Will the director, the SM, or an actor lead in warm-ups and will everyone be expected to participate?
   - How many rehearsals will be spent discussing and reading the script?
   - How many will be needed for **blocking** (planning the actors' movements)?
   - Will the director preblock or allow improvisation to preceed and/or lead blocking?

- When should the actors be **off-book** (know their lines and blocking) and how should you correct lines and blocking?
- When will rehearsal props be needed and when will they be replaced by production props?
- Will there be differences in procedure when refining rehearsals begin?
- How are tardy and absent actors to be dealt with and who does it?

8. Finalize the rehearsal schedule and production calendar and provide copies to the staff. The rehearsal calendar should always be labeled as "tentative" since it may have to be adjusted to suit the progress of the rehearsals or any number of unexpected crises. It should include:

- time and place for each rehearsal
- scenes to be rehearsed
- dates for actors to be off-book
- deadlines for rehearsal props to be available
- deadlines for dances and combat to be up to performance level

NOTE: Schedule plenty of time for fight rehearsals. It takes time to bring fight choreography up to tempo and to then integrate characterization, dialogue and bystanders. Demand the time necessary to assure quality and safety in performance.

The production calendar, due to the amount of information it will include, can be a hand-drawn or photo-enlarged version of the six-weeks calendar. After completing the calendar you can reduce it for individual use, saving the large version to post on the callboard. The production calendar should include dates and deadlines for all aspects of the show that can be scheduled at this time, such as:

- dates for various phases of rehearsals (reading, blocking, **run-throughs,** technical)
- dates for publicity shoots
- deadlines for scenery, costume, and lighting designs
- deadlines for scenery and costume completion
- deadline for poster completion
- dates for "loading out" and "loading in" the show
- performance dates

If the rehearsal period lasts longer than six weeks, the calendar may be edited to add time (sample p. 20).

9. Read through the script again. Make a *script breakdown* (p. 85), a *character breakdown* (p. 86), and a *prop breakdown* (p. 87). You will need input

and approval from the director for all three forms. Fill out a *rehearsal props request* (p. 88) and a *rehearsal costumes request* (p. 89) and get approval from the director on both. Rehearsal props may be limited to furniture or other set props which define space until the actors are off-book.

10. Deliver the rehearsal costumes and props request forms to the costume and properties masters/mistresses. Ask about special care and handling for these props and costumes. Store them in a convenient lockable space and tape a copy of each of these lists inside the door of the storage space for easy check-off after each rehearsal.

11. Deliver the list of rehearsal weapons and fight gear (masks, gloves, padding, etc.) to the fight director (or props master/mistress) and get instructions for their care and handling. Store them with the other props and costumes, or separately if requested. Weapons should be assigned to one person for care and handling. The inherent danger in these props demands separate and knowledgeable care. There are special guidelines for stage managing stage combat in Chapter 5 which include the care and handling of weapons.

12. Get a loose-leaf notebook large enough to accommodate your rehearsal script and all relevant paperwork (see Chapter 3).

13. Meet with the designer or technical director (TD) to go over the **ground plan** for the scenery. Do not be afraid to ask *any* questions. Much time can be wasted by a misinterpretation of technical drawings. Tape the ground plan on the rehearsal floor. If it is your first time to tape a plan, you may need the assistance of the designer or technical director. You will certainly need at least one ASM or PA to help with measuring. Instructions for taping a ground plan are in Appendix D. Photographically reduce a copy of the ground plan to fit your production book (8 1/2″ × 11″).

14. Prepare information packets that include the following items for each cast member:

   ■ a script (if they have not already picked one up)
   ■ research information from the dramaturg or director
   ■ a contact sheet
   ■ a rehearsal schedule
   ■ a *publicity sheet* (p. 90)
   ■ a copy of the health and safety guidelines for your company and theatre
   ■ any relevant Equity forms
   ■ and a copy of the company rules (see Appendix C; some theatres have their own written standard of expectations for actors)

15. Make a list of emergency and maintenance telephone numbers. Put one copy in your production book and post one in the rehearsal space.

16. Post information for the first rehearsal using the *rehearsal call* form (p. 91).

READING REHEARSALS

The first rehearsals include the entire cast, and future rehearsals may be divided into smaller groups—for a long time. Consequently, this is the best opportunity for getting production business done. Carefully schedule the following: the publicist may want to get approval of program listings and biographies and schedule interviews; the producer may wish to talk to the cast and finalize contracts, insurance, or employment forms; the costumer may want to get measurements and schedule fittings; and the designer may wish to present a model of the scenery. If you have Equity actors, an Equity meeting must be held. During this closed meeting, other actors can fill out forms, be measured for costumes, and so on. In the absence of the above mentioned personnel, you may have to conduct all of this business yourself.

This is also the best time to address rules and regulations which will govern rehearsals and to establish an atmosphere of creativity and commitment. A production company is a family and the most important guidelines in keeping the family productive are communication and consideration. If you have company rules, read through them on the first night. For a sample of company rules, refer to Appendix C.

Cast members hold an informal text discussion during an early rehearsal of *Cabaret* at the University of Iowa. (Photo by David Conklin)

Include warm-ups even in these early rehearsals to relieve stress, allow emotional and intellectual focus, and simply to begin a physical and spiritual communication within the cast.

At reading rehearsals the cast may sit at desks or around a table and make notes in their script while reading it. This is a time when the director can discuss interpretation, characterization, pronunciation, structural beats, divisions into **French scenes,** and so on. You should bring a standard dictionary for definitions and a pronouncing dictionary which uses the International Phonetic Alphabet (**IPA**). If you cannot use the IPA, assign an ASM or actor to this task.

Make a copy of the *reading rehearsals checklist* (p. 46), edit it to suit the production, and use it as a guide.

1. The SM staff should always be *early* for each rehearsal and have the space prepared so that rehearsals can begin at the time called.

2. Sweep the rehearsal floor, checking for hazards, before and after all rehearsals especially if this space is also used for scenery construction. Actors are often required to sit or lie on the floor, go without shoes, or practice combat or dance. A wet or slippery floor, nails, screws, or splinters can badly injure an actor as well as interrupt and delay rehearsals.

3. Adjust the room temperature to an appropriate level of comfort and arrange for drinking water. If there is no water fountain, a cooler may be needed. Often juice and/or coffee are also expected at rehearsals. Many people today drink only decaffeinated coffee or tea. Have both available.

4. Post no-smoking signs where appropriate and respect the requests of those who cannot work in smoke-filled rooms due to allergies or a concern for their health. There must be a consistency in this rule for staff, crew, and performers. Company rules should spell out the restrictions and consequences. Balance these restrictions by providing a space where smokers can take breaks.

5. Most directors prefer closed rehearsals (no visitors unless approved). Post signs on all entrances to the rehearsal space to inform uninvited guests of the policy.

6. Post a *sign-in sheet* (p. 92) and instruct actors to sign it upon arrival. Sign-in sheets allow the ASM to see that all actors are present without searching the building. No one should ever **sign in** for someone else.

7. If an actor has not arrived at the scheduled time, telephone. Using a neutral tone, ask the actor if he/she is coming to rehearsal and get an estimated time of arrival. Politely request that the actor telephone the next time he/she must be late. For continued tardiness or missed rehearsals, follow procedures defined in the company rules or determined by the director. Some companies dismiss actors for abuse of these rules; others assess monetary fines. Be sure these procedures have been addressed in an early rehearsal.

8. Give out the script/information packets to the cast and set a deadline for completing the publicity sheet. Review the company rules (Appendix C).

9. Establish the times set for breaks. If there are Equity people in your rehearsals, the number and length of break times are prescribed for them in the AEA rule book.

10. Schedule appointments for fittings, photos, and so on.

11. Review the company's health and safety regulations (see Chapter 7). Demonstrate use of fire extinguishers, locate the fire exits, and review procedures for emergency evacuations. Find out who is first-aid certified.

12. Maintain a *production log* (p. 93). These are notes taken at each rehearsal usually consisting of the rehearsal agenda and reminders of things to do or messages to artistic or technical staff. Write down and date everything.

13. Read for absent actors and note any script changes.

14. Secure the space after each rehearsal.

BLOCKING AND REFINING REHEARSALS

Blocking rehearsals are for planning the movement of the actors and the use of stage space and are often slow and tedious. The director may have everything planned on paper or in his/her head. However, as the actors move through the plan, the director may adjust and change as the need arises. Other directors block spontaneously, allowing the actors much freedom in contributing ideas. Either way, you will need good notation skills (see Chapter 4) and several erasers.

Assuming you are beginning with a good script and a talented cast and staff, the final quality of the production rests on the time available for refining. Assurance of that time for the director is your responsibility. Make the reading and blocking rehearsals move smoothly and quickly by avoiding unnecessary delays due to poor communication, lack of organization, or inaccurate notations.

Refining rehearsals are for tuning up the movement, characterization, pacing, and intensity of the show. It is an exciting time of exploration, discovery, and development, and it requires sensitivity, openness, and trust from each person involved in the process.

> *In preparing the rehearsal of a scene with nudity, you may schedule a conference with the director and the involved actor(s) to discuss the scene. Consider the actor's preference in scheduling closed rehearsals. In my experience, most actors just want to get on with rehearsals and not call attention to the nude scenes. . . . just do them. . . . without a lot of fuss.*
>
> —CRAIG WEINDLING, AEA STAGE MANAGER

A student stage manager confers with the director while taking notes during an audition at North Carolina Central University. (Photo by J. B. Alston)

Make a copy of the *blocking and refining rehearsals checklist* (p. 47), edit it to suit the production, and use it as a guide.

1. Continue the same preparation rituals established in the first rehearsals: arrive early; provide a safe and comfortable rehearsal environment; maintain the callboard; and post all rehearsal schedule changes.

   Continue the same rehearsal activities: respond to tardiness and absenteeism; call and time breaks; remind actors of appointments such as costume fittings, publicity shoots, or individual rehearsals; and maintain the production log.

2. Reserve a desk or hard surface for your use. You should sit in front of the acting area. If rehearsals are in the theatre, there may be room for a desk in front of the first rows of seats or you may prefer to sit farther back, requiring a portable table top. The table should be large enough to accommodate your open production book, an additional writing pad, and a lamp (if lighting is poor).

3. If you are working with an adapted or original script, make copies of any changes, date them and distribute them to the cast and staff. Above all, keep your production book up-to-date.

Director Randolph Umberger (right) gives blocking instructions to actors (right to left) Diane Fuller, Tom Marriott, and Robert Beatty during a blocking rehearsal for *I'm Not Rappaport.* (Photo by J. B. Alston)

4. **Spike the set props** by taping their positions on the stage floor. This is done to guide the stage crew in the placement of furniture and other moveable props. For instructions on spiking set props, refer to Appendix E.

5. Run warm-ups according to the director's, choreographer's, and fight director's specifications. The **dance captain** will warm up dancers, and the **fight captain** will warm up fighters.

6. Blocking rehearsals are tedious and demanding. Actors will write their own blocking in their scripts. You must note everyone's blocking in the production book (see Chapter 4 for instructions). When there are nine or more characters in a scene and blocking may be difficult to keep up with, you may ask an ASM to help track particular characters. After rehearsal you can get together to compare notes and add those you missed to your production book.

   Inform actors when they deviate from the correct blocking. They may have written the wrong directions or they may have neglected to note a change. Your book must be accurate. If it is not, make changes and move on. Ask the director for his/her preferred procedure on correcting blocking. You may be expected to give a starting place each time rehearsal resumes after a correction. Poorly done, this can delay a rehearsal and cause frustration for everyone.

7. Call technical cues such as **blackouts,** door bells, telephone rings, or other lighting or sound effects that cue movements or lines. If taped sound

effects are available, integrate them as early as possible. One of the ASMs can be assigned to run the tape player.

8. Once the actors are off-book, ask the director for his/her preferred method of prompting. This is a good job for an ASM, as you need to continue concentrating on the accuracy of the actors' blocking. There are several methods for prompting: You may be asked to wait for an actor to call for a forgotten line; you may be asked to give the line in the character's voice; you may be asked to use a neutral voice, avoiding interpretation; you may be asked to give only the first one or two words of the line; or you may be asked to give the entire line.

   NOTE: Do not let your voice communicate impatience, sarcasm, or any other judgement quality when prompting an actor.

   Soon after actors are off-book, begin making line notes (writing down the lines that are dropped or changed and giving them to the actors after rehearsal).

9. Continue collecting program information. Use the *program acknowledgments* form (p. 94) to credit individuals or businesses for any assistance with the production.

10. Make *dance sheets* (p. 95) and *combat sheets* (p. 96) as needed. These sheets will assist you in scheduling separate rehearsals and will be of use to the choreographer, the fight director, and the costumer.

11. Rehearse the understudies without interrupting the regular flow of rehearsals. Whenever possible, rehearse them with the actors they will play opposite. Understudies should attend all rehearsals which involve their character. They will learn lines and blocking by taking their own notes and observing. One excellent way for an understudy to learn lines is by running lines with other actors. This helps the other actors to learn their own lines and to feel comfortable with the understudy the first time they have to appear on stage. It may be your responsibility to prepare the understudy for the role. Resist the temptation to redirect. Your responsibility is to communicate the same guidelines the director gave to the original actor. Understudies are charged with the difficult task of learning the interpretation of the actor they may have to replace because a change in interpretation might throw the rest of the cast off.

12. Respond to injuries or emergencies following guidelines in Chapter 7. Use the *accident report* (p. 97) to document circumstances of any injury. This information may assist the physician that ultimately treats the victim as well as provide statistics for a question of liability.

13. Obtain costume plots for each actor from the costumer and advise the costumer of any quick changes. The speed needed in putting on or taking off a costume may influence design and building decisions.

14. Invite the production staff and crews to an early run-through. Their familiarity with the show will make technical rehearsals run smoother.

     When refining rehearsals begin, use a stopwatch to time scenes, acts, run-throughs, and breaks.

15. Organize and run the costume parade if one is required. The purpose of the costume parade is to allow the director and costumer to see the actors in costume, preferably under stage lights. Try to make the parade run quickly and smoothly, but be sure the director and costumer are through evaluating a costume before you ask an actor to change. Costumes that are to be worn together must be seen together.

16. As soon as the program information is typed, post a copy on the callboard for cast, staff, and crew to proofread. Give corrections to the publicist.

17. Make a list of any additional performance props and submit it to the props master/mistress. Using the *borrowed items record* (p. 98) and the *rented items record* (p. 99), document, document, document.

18. Request make-up designs including estimates on the time needed to carry out each design. Complex make-up may require an earlier call or additional personnel.

19. Be sure that all notes from rehearsals are communicated to production departments and follow up to see that the notes are being followed.

     Lock up costumes, props, and rehearsal space after each rehearsal. If the space will be used between rehearsals, find another lockable room or closet for the costumes and props.

NOTE: Unless you are an expert in the area, do not pass on solutions. Pass on problems. Let the appropriate department address the best way to solve the problems.

TECHNICAL REHEARSALS

In technical rehearsals, maintain a sense of humor and a positive attitude, playing down a sense of crisis and instilling confidence in the final product.

—CHRIS JONES, NORTHERN ILLINOIS UNIVERSITY

Technical rehearsals are for integrating the **scenery**, sound, lights, and other special effects which are a part of the total production. As the number of rehearsal staff and crew personnel multiply, demands on your organizational skills will reach a peak.

In opera, many cues are divided between the stage manager and the assistant conductor who cues the orchestra and backstage chorus.

—MING CHO LEE, YALE SCHOOL OF DRAMA

If the production has more technical and acting cues than one person can call with efficiency, assign a backstage ASM to give acting calls (warnings and entrances, backstage sound effects, etc.) or have one or two technicians (such as the follow spot operator) work independently, using visual cues. If none of these approaches work, look for another solution. Keep in your control those cues which are significant to timing.

> *Timing is everything. I need musically sensitive stage managers. It helps if they read music and are* musical *(not one who plays an instrument, but who can* feel *the music). Stage Managers have caused disasters when they called the show in an erratic, non-musical way.*
>
> —GERALD FREEDMAN, NORTH CAROLINA SCHOOL OF THE ARTS
> AND GREAT LAKES THEATRE FESTIVAL

This chapter includes basic guidelines for calling a show, but more detailed information appears in Appendix E.

Prior to and during technical rehearsals,

- prepare the cast by explaining the technical rehearsal process and schedule; communicate the same to the staff and crews
- know the names of the attending staff and running crews; try to anticipate ways to assist them
- project a positive attitude; compliment good work and be patient with mistakes; discourage negativity and defensiveness in response to criticism

If you will be working with union crews, become familiar with their guidelines. Know the minimum time and overtime regulations as well as anything else that might affect the flow of rehearsals.

Make a copy of the *technical rehearsals checklist* (p. 48), edit it to suit the production, and use it as a guide only. *Now is the time to be cool and flexible.*

1. Confer with the technical director (TD) to set times for the production **running crews** to meet.

    Assist with the **load-in** (moving scenery, props, and costumes from the rehearsal space to the theatre). Ask the TD for specific needs at load-in and help make the process as smooth as possible. If actors are assisting with the load-in, avoid giving them duties which might lead to injury.

2. Supervise the arrangement of the **scene dock** (storage space in wings and backstage for props and scenery). Movement of scenery and props is often done in view of the audience and requires choreography in order to make it smooth and efficient. For this reason, where a prop or piece of scenery is stored can be very important to the running of the scene change. You will probably need to confer with the director and the TD about this task. Fill out the *preset plot* (p. 100) and the *shift plot* (p. 101). Post copies of these completed forms backstage.

> *NOTE: Be sure to keep entrances and exits open and clearly marked so that actors can move through them in character and with no fear of injury.*

Arrange the **prop tables.** Hand props, which are brought on or off by the actors and which are moved on or off during scene changes, are usually stored backstage on long tables. See Appendix E for the traditional method. Post a *prop sheet* (p. 102) on the wall above the prop table, listing props, which are scheduled to be on that side of the stage.

3. If quick costume changes must be made backstage, reserve a space for this to happen and post a *costume change plot* (p. 103) in that location for each actor using it. A dresser should be assigned to assist in quick changes.

4. Make sure dressing rooms have been cleaned and stocked with appropriate supplies.

Assign dressing rooms and post sign-in sheets in them. Often there are only two rooms—one for men and one for women. However, if you have a cast with an unbalanced ratio of women to men, you may need to

Stage technicians review the paper tech for *Cabaret.* Paper techs are often held in the theatre where a view of the stage and scenery can assist in the planning. (Photo by David Conklin)

find a third room for the smaller group and let the larger group use both of the dressing rooms.

5.   Set up the **cue** communication system. Your system may include a stage manager's console or simply a limited number of headsets. If you have options, locate your calling position where you will be most effective. A console has a light panel, which provides cues for scene changes, entrances, the **fly deck,** and so on. Also, there are channels for verbal communication with each station. Because light and sound cues are given verbally, many stage managers prefer to be in the **control booth** where they are not dependent on the reliability of headsets to communicate with the **board operator** and the **sound technician.** This also frees you to focus on the timing and execution of cues without the distraction of backstage traffic. However, if you do not have a trained staff, you may need to be located in a more accessible space than the control booth.

6.   **Paper tech** is the first phase of technical rehearsals and involves the director, SM staff, TD, lighting and sound designers, and all running crews. At this meeting, all technical cues are listed in order. Get a copy of the *lighting instrument schedule* from the TD. It identifies where instruments are hung and the area they service. It will be valuable for troubleshooting and for touring. Provide the lighting and sound technicians with appropriate **cue sheets** (*light cue sheet*, p. 104; *follow spot cue sheet*, p. 105; *sound cue sheet*, p. 106). Use the generic *cue sheet* (p. 107) for other technicians working the production and for your master list of cues. As with blocking notes, technicians write only their own cues while you note all cues. How the cues will be numbered is based on the type of communication system you have for calling the show. For a more thorough discussion on numbering cues, refer to Appendix F.

In some large houses, every designer is at a computer, putting their cues into memory rather than on paper.

—CAROL CLARK, AEA STAGE MANAGER

7.   Make a list of preshow checks on technical equipment. The TD can assist you in setting up a procedure which fits the equipment used in your production. The *dimmer/instrument check* (p. 108) is used for stage lights.

NOTE: There are many different light and sound systems in use today. Your equipment may be controlled manually or by computer. Therefore, cue sheets may have to be adapted to suit the equipment and its use in your production.

8.   Set up spotting lights (blue lights that help actors get off stage during a blackout) and use flourescent tape on stairs or any place where an actor may have to move in a blackout. Low-wattage lamps may be needed for backstage workers: The prop tables may need to be lighted, difficult exit

stairs or ramps may need lights, and so on. If the lights can be seen by the audience, aim them in another direction and/or tape a piece of blue gel in front of the light source.

9. Meet with the backstage running crew to choreograph scenery and prop **shifts.** Be sure positions for scenery and props are properly spiked (see Appendix E). Assign headsets and if they are battery operated, be sure there are spare batteries accessible. Rehearse scene shifts, using the level of lighting that will be available during performances.

10. **Dry tech** is for the SM and crews to run through the show without the actors. It may also be referred to as a *dry run.* This will be your first opportunity to "call" the show. It is especially important to practice the opening of the show. Usually, there is preshow music which must fade or an overture which is played by an orchestra; lights in the house (seating area) which go to half intensity and then out; and the curtain rises as stage lights come on. The procedure varies with the production. Many directors choose not to use a front curtain.

To call a cue you will ideally have time to give:

- a **warning** at least one minute before time for the execution of the cue
- a **stand by** a few lines of dialogue before the cue
- and a **go** at the moment the effect should begin

> Example: light cue 23, warning
>
> light cue 23, stand by
>
> light cue 23, go

NOTE: If there are many cues in a short period of time, you may need to eliminate the stand-by *cue. For more detailed information on the procedure for calling a show, refer to Appendix F.*

11. **Cue-to-cue** is a run-through with actors skipping in dialogue from one technical cue to the next in order to set volume and intensity levels. The director or lighting designer or TD sits in the audience with a headset and communicates with the SM about these decisions and about the timing for cues. If characters are involved in the opening cues, use as much time as allowable to set these cues and practice them. *Of Mules and Men* was performed at the Kennedy Center as part of the American College Theatre Festival. The opening of the play always drew applause and was very dependent on timing. It began with the stage lights at a very low level and the **house lights** at half; the characters entered one at a time, wordlessly greeting one another, establishing relationships and then freezing in a characteristic pose; when the last character struck his pose, house lights went out as stage lights came up on a richly informative tableau.

This student stage manager calls cues for a production of *The Fantasticks* staged at Northern Illinois University. (Photo by George Tarbay)

Whatever the procedure is, practice it. It must be smooth. It sets the tone for the rest of the production and establishes your technical professionalism to the audience.

12. **Full tech** is a complete run-through of the production with all technical effects. It may not include the curtain call (when actors take their bows) as some directors like to wait until a dress rehearsal to choreograph this.

> *NOTE: After each technical rehearsal, all technical production area heads should meet with the SM and director to review notes on tech and to discuss corrections or changes.*

13. **Final dress** is the last rehearsal before opening night and often allows for an invited audience. With or without an audience, it should be treated exactly like a performance so there will be no surprises on opening night. Take no short-cuts. Do everything from preshow music to the final curtain. All running crews and stage managers should dress in black to prevent them from being visible to the audience and to make them less noticeable during scene changes. Require this clothing tradition on the night of final dress rehearsal.

14. One ASM should be responsible for collecting actors' valuables, locking them up in a safe place before dress rehearsals and performances, and returning them at the end of the rehearsal or performance. It is best if each actor has a container labeled with his/her name, rather than putting everyone's valuables together.

15. Make a **comp** (complimentary ticket) list for crews and cast and turn it in to the box office manager.

16. Time scenes, acts, intermissions, and the full production using the *stage manager's report* (p. 109). This form is vitally important. Be thorough and honest. The director needs to know about each problem, when it occured, and how it was addressed so that he/she will know how to solve it and prevent it from reoccuring.

    Take technical and performance notes and give them to those they concern after each rehearsal.

17. Post *repair sheets* (p. 110) backstage (for scenery and props) and in the dressing rooms (for costumes), instruct the actors and running crew on how to use them and notify crew chiefs of needed repairs. Check the next day to see that they have been done.

18. Teach each ASM to call the show in case of an emergency. Regardless of your commitment, there are times when you cannot go on with the show, so it must be able to go on without you. One stage manager told how she was carried kicking and screaming from the theatre and rushed to the hospital for an emergency appendectomy. Your cues should be so clearly written that anyone could read them and call the show.

NOTE: If you are working with inexperienced students or volunteers, they are not going to learn the vocabulary, or the skills in one tech rehearsal. Be patient.

PERFORMANCES

It is now time for the magic to commence and for everyone to reap the rewards of many weeks of effort. The director and designers can sit back and enjoy the show or check in to a hospital for their breakdown. Their job is basically finished. Your job moves into high gear. With the exit of the director, you become completely responsible for running the show. However, if you have been well organized and thorough in rehearsals, the rest of the production can be satisfying and even uplifting.

Opening night is the goal of all the previous work. Everyone should be a little tense. It keeps you on your toes, ready to respond to unexpected emergencies, which will occur, no matter how well you have planned. Avoid taking

The production of *I'm Not Rappaport* is presented on stage at North Carolina Central University. Director for the play was Randolph Umberger and designer was Doris Schneider. (Photo by J. B. Alston)

medications or libations which will slow your reactions. Everyone is depending on your clarity of mind and control of the show.

Mistakes will be made. That is inevitable. Although you may not make the mistake, you will probably have to correct it. Some errors cannot be anticipated; some can. Think through potential problem areas and have a plan of action in mind. For example, if you are in the middle of a show and someone on stage drops a whole tray of glasses, what would you do? Would you bring the curtain in? Would you have a prop crew ready to sweep it up? Or would you have an appropriate character (such as a parent or a maid/custodian) come in and clean up the floor, "in character"? You will establish your level of professionalism not by how few mistakes are made but by how effectively they are corrected or covered.

You can change the whole pace of the show by the way you communicate, even when calling cues. This is especially important for a long-running show where boredom and moods can influence timing and performance. If you are negative, the whole crew will feel negative, so it is very important for you, as the stage manager, to be consistent and positive.

Following each performance, report any major problems to the appropriate staff person. If necessary, get help in solving them and preventing them from happening again.

Make a copy of the *performance checklist* (p. 49), edit it to suit the production, and use it as a guide. Your focus during performances is to call the show and to problem-solve.

1. All of the SM staff should be in the theatre at least one hour before curtain time (when play begins).

    Create and follow a preshow checklist which includes checking the **stage** and **house** (the audience seating area) for performance readiness.

2. Synchronize watches with the house manager and set a time or signal for opening the house to the audience. The **house manager** may wear a headset to coordinate opening the house, curtain time, and intermission.

3. Call for a lighting, sound, and cueing check. You may need to assist with the light check if there is only one board operator. The purpose is to make sure all instruments are functioning properly. If an instrument is not functioning, correct the problem, replace the instrument, or plan how to work without it. The **sound technician** should check the sound equipment and have the first cue ready to begin. Check all headsets and be sure there are spare batteries at each location where a headset is to be used. Loss of communication with an ASM or running crew during performance can lead to a technical disaster.

4. Check scenery and props which have been **preset** for the first scene. Look backstage to see that all remaining props and scenery are in their assigned places. Your preshow checks serve to assure you that everything is in place and functioning.

    Last minute additions, changes, or repairs to the scenery and props may create surprises or hazards for actors and crew. Look for any changes and relay the information or walk them through the area if necessary to make them fully aware of how the changes will affect them.

    I performed in Sly Fox *in a production which was technically behind schedule. On opening night, I pounded on the scenery door, felt pain in my hand, but ignored it and made my entrance in character. In the middle of the scene, I wiped my brow which was followed by a gasp from the audience. There was a mixture of blood and black paint on my face. An alert stage manager would have checked new scenery for exposed nails and warned actors of fresh paint.*

    —ERIC FORSYTHE, UNIVERSITY OF IOWA

5. The booth and **backstage** areas should be clear of anyone other than crew members assigned to those positions and actors waiting for an entrance.

6. Check sign-in sheets at a specified time and telephone late actors. If a missing actor cannot be reached, prepare the understudy. If the actor shows up at the last moment, follow company policy as to whether the understudy or the original actor performs. Do not make a bad situation

worse by reacting with anger. You can discuss the lateness or the absence after the show. Sending an embarrassed or angry actor on stage can negatively influence everyone's performance.

If an actor must be replaced, instruct the house manager to post the change in the lobby, and arrange for someone to announce the change from the stage.

7. Give time calls to the actors and crews: "thirty minutes," "fifteen minutes," "five minutes," and "places" are standard but other preplanned warnings can be used. This can be done through the headset if there are monitors in the dressing rooms and **green room** (lounge for actors). Otherwise, have an ASM announce the warnings.

8. Coordinate with the house manager on curtain time, intermission, and so on. You may have to hold the curtain if the audience is still being seated.

9. Call cues, monitor the show (take notes on performance and tech), time each act and the intermission(s), and anticipate and solve problems.

10. Supervise scene shifts. If you are in the control booth, this must be done by the backstage SM or ASM.

11. If the **grand drape** is used and is drawn rather than lowered and raised, assign an ASM or PA to oversee its proper closure and to prevent it from hitting any stage props. The procedure for doing this is to walk beside and behind the curtain as it is being drawn, moving obstacles which might have been dropped or moved too far downstage. It also allows the person **walking the curtain** to make sure it closes completely so that actors frozen in position can move and prop shifts can begin.

12. Fill out the stage manager's report, have the house manager review and sign it, give a copy to the director or producer, and keep the original in your production book.

Following each performance, the standard practice is to set up the stage for the next one. However, if the stage is to be used for another purpose before the next performance, you may have to clear it.

13. Give acting and crew notes after each performance. These notes may address such things as dropped lines, changes in blocking or interpretation, errors in set or prop changes, poorly timed responses to called cues, and so on.

Following a performance of Phantom of the Opera *in San Francisco, I had the opportunity to observe the stage manager giving notes to the cast. The notes were extensive, commenting on acting nuances and style, not just blocking and lines.*

—CHRIS JONES, NORTHERN ILLINOIS UNIVERSITY

14. Check repair sheets each evening after the performance and follow up on maintenance of scenery, props, and costumes. Do not depend solely on others to let you know when a repair is needed. Keep a watchful eye on the

condition of scenery, props, lights, and costumes. If the company is paying for repairs, try to get as many done at once as possible rather than calling crews in numerous times for individual or minor adjustments. Pay particular attention to any scenery, prop, or technical equipment that poses a potential hazard for actors or crews.

15. Get a *photo list* (p. 111) for the production photographer. Organize the shoot so actors will know when they are to be in which costume. Supervise the shoot.

16. If you are managing a long-running show, maintenance of the cast morale is important. Weariness (especially if the actors have other jobs), boredom due to repetition, and the usual personality conflicts can create breaches in the spirit of family and can affect the quality of the production. Be alert to these problems and look for solutions. Organize activities (such as cookouts, athletic games, picnics, etc.) So much time is spent inside a windowless theatre in the preparation and the performing of a play, that outdoor activities are often the ones most appreciated.

17. Run **brush-up rehearsals** as needed, usually following a long break in performances or if the actors' timing, blocking, or characterizations seem to be changing inappropriately. Audience reactions such as laughter at an **ad-libbed** piece of **stage business** can influence an actor's next performance. This can alter cues and interpretation by other actors sharing the scene. Watch for such changes and correct them.

    Continue to rehearse understudies and (if it is a long-running show) you may be needed to block and rehearse replacement actors. Remember, in each of these situations, you are responsible for maintaining the integrity of the director's interpretation of the script.

18. Most educational companies videotape their productions. If the videotape is used for anything other than company archives, be aware of copyright laws. Also, if you have any Equity actors, be aware of the Equity guidelines concerning videotaping their performances.

    Be sure the videotaping crew and equipment are set up before the audience is seated and that they cause as little distraction to the audience as possible. Do not wait until the last performance to videotape. If something goes wrong, you will need another opportunity to do it right.

POSTPRODUCTION

At the close of a production, it will either be toured, temporarily stored for a future tour, or *struck* (all scenery, props, and costumes returned to the lender, stored as stock material, dismantled, or discarded). The **load-out** (removal of the show from the theatre) must be organized with the next step in mind.

If the scenery is to be reassembled, label everything, even braces. Make sketches of any **masking** or support, which may not appear on the original drawings. If it is to be transported by truck to another theatre, the load-out should be carefully planned so that the load-in follows a logical sequence. In other words, the last things loaded should be the first things you need when unloading. The TD may make these decisions or run the load-out with your assistance. Make checklists of all scenery, props, and costumes being loaded and take care not to remove furniture or equipment that belongs to the theatre which you are leaving. Double-check to see that everything has been loaded.

We arrived at the Kennedy Center with Of Mules and Men *to find the stage manager had overlooked two set props—a bench and a chair (still sitting beside the loading dock three hundred miles away).*

—RANDOLPH UMBERGER, NORTH CAROLINA CENTRAL UNIVERSITY

If the show is to be temporarily stored in another space to await a later tour, follow the same steps. Store the show in a lockable space after all care and maintenance has been completed for the next performance.

If the production is over (not to be revived), you will schedule a **strike**. More than a clearing of the stage, a strike of a completed production involves storing, returning, and/or cleaning all scenery, props, and costumes as well as cleaning the stage, rehearsal space, dressing rooms, and shop. The strike is usually held immediately following the final curtain of the last performance in order to clear the theatre for an incoming show. While the actors are mourning, partying, or sleeping, you and the crews will be working. This is not the case with all companies, however: Many actors are willing and even expected to participate. Sometimes the strike can be delayed, allowing everyone to participate in both the end-of-show parties and the load-out.

Make a copy of the *postproduction checklist* (p. 50), edit it to suit the production, and use it as a guide.

1. Post strike information several days in advance. The procedure will vary from one company to another. Educational and community theatres often have a strike party. The strike is followed by refreshments and celebration.

2. Assist with the strike: Borrowed or rented props should be returned to the owner; stock props should be returned to storage; costumes should be washed or cleaned before they are returned to the owners or storage; make-up should be stored or claimed (for hygienic reasons, most actors provide their own make-up unless the design requires special products); the dressing rooms, stage, backstage, and shop should be cleared and cleaned.

3. Return keys and follow up on any other paperwork, such as turning in the petty cash accounting sheet and receipts.

4. Clean up your production book. Ask the producer/director if the theatre wishes to retain a copy for their archives or for future revivals of the show. Keep a copy for yourself: It can become a part of your portfolio.

5. Send thank-you letters and a copy of the program to each person listed in the acknowledgements.

6. If appropriate, request letters of recommendation for your portfolio. Contacts and impressions made during a production can lead to future employment. Stage management is a position of trust and expressions of confidence by respected theatre artists will open doors.

7. Update your resumé. Refer to Chapter 8 for recommendations for resumé format and content.

PREPRODUCTION CHECKLIST

Play _____

SM _____

_____ 1.   Edit and make working copies of production forms relevant to your show.

_____ 2.   Order scripts.

_____ 3.   Read and evaluate the script.

_____ 4.   Number scripts and maintain the list of borrowers.

_____ 5.   Review information on the performance space.

_____ 6.   Meet with the director to discuss the production.

_____ 7.   Meet with the SM staff and assign duties.

_____ 8.   Schedule the first production meeting and notify the staff.

_____ 9.   Participate in the first production meeting.

_____ 10. Plan how auditions will be run and procure needed props.

_____ 11. Edit and make copies of the audition form.

_____ 12. Prepare and post the audition notices.

_____ 13. Get copies of all keys needed for the production.

_____ 14. Reserve the audition room(s).

_____ 15. Prepare the audition space and post audition information.

_____ 16. Locate and update the SM's kit.

_____ 17. Request petty cash, record-keeping procedures, and budget allocations.

_____ 18. Arrange for a desk for your use between rehearsals.

_____ 19. _____

Harcourt Brace & Company

AUDITION CHECKLIST

Play _____

SM _____

_____ 1. *Inspect the space and post signs to aid in the flow of auditions.*

_____ 2. *Assign and position staff to facilitate the flow of auditions.*

_____ 3. *Mark the stage floor if a limited space is spotlighted for auditions.*

_____ 4. *Take notes for the director and maintain the paperwork.*

_____ 5. *After auditions, secure props and reorganize the space.*

_____ 6. *Post the callbacks and information on time and place.*

_____ 7. *Manage callbacks.*

_____ 8. *Post the cast list and first rehearsal call.*

_____ 9. *Assign scripts.*

_____ 10. _____

_____ 11. _____

_____ 12. _____

_____ 13. _____

_____ 14. _____

_____ 15. _____

_____ 16. _____

_____ 17. _____

_____ 18. _____

_____ 19. _____

Harcourt Brace & Company

Play _____

PREREHEARSAL
CHECKLIST

SM _____

_____ 1.   *Prepare and maintain the callboard.*

_____ 2.   *Post blank schedule forms for actors and a deadline for their return.*

_____ 3.   *Get completed schedule forms from the production staff.*

_____ 4.   *Make a contact sheet and distribute copies.*

_____ 5.   *Determine the rehearsal space.*

_____ 6.   *Get information for maintaining the rehearsal space.*

_____ 7.   *Meet with the director for rehearsal schedule and guidelines.*

_____ 8.   *Finalize calendars; post and distribute copies.*

_____ 9.   *Complete script evaluation forms and rehearsal prop and costume request forms.*

_____ 10. *Collect and store rehearsal costumes and props.*

_____ 11. *Collect rehearsal weapons and assign their care to one person.*

_____ 12. *Prepare the production book.*

_____ 13. *Tape the ground plan to the rehearsal floor.*

_____ 14. *Prepare handouts for the cast.*

_____ 15. *Prepare a list of emergency phone numbers.*

_____ 16. *Post information for the first rehearsal.*

_____ 17. _____

_____ 18. _____

_____ 19. _____

Harcourt Brace & Company

READING
REHEARSALS
CHECKLIST

Play _____

SM _____

_____ 1. *Arrive early and prepare the rehearsal space.*

_____ 2. *Sweep and check the floor for hazards.*

_____ 3. *Adjust the room temperature and arrange for drinking water.*

_____ 4. *Post signs to identify smoking and nonsmoking areas.*

_____ 5. *If rehearsals are closed, post signs.*

_____ 6. *Post the sign-in sheet for actors.*

_____ 7. *Telephone late cast or rehearsal personnel.*

_____ 8. *Distribute the script/information packets and review company rules.*

_____ 9. *Set break times.*

_____ 10. *Schedule appointments for fittings and/or photos.*

_____ 11. *Review health and safety regulations and emergency procedures.*

_____ 12. *Maintain a production log.*

_____ 13. *Read for absent actors and note script changes.*

_____ 14. *Secure the space after each rehearsal.*

_____ 15. _____

_____ 16. _____

_____ 17. _____

_____ 18. _____

_____ 19. _____

Harcourt Brace & Company

BLOCKING AND REFINING REHEARSALS CHECKLIST

Play
_____

SM
_____

_____ 1. *Continue preparation rituals and rehearsal activities.*

_____ 2. *Reserve a desk or portable hard surface for your rehearsal use.*

_____ 3. *Note, copy, and distribute any script changes.*

_____ 4. *Spike the set props.*

_____ 5. *Run or assign the running of warm-ups.*

_____ 6. *Note all blocking and correct actors' blocking.*

_____ 7. *Call or execute technical cues.*

_____ 8. *Prompt actors and take line notes.*

_____ 9. *Collect program information including acknowledgments.*

_____ 10. *Fill out dance and combat sheets if they are needed.*

_____ 11. *Rehearse understudies.*

_____ 12. *Respond to injuries or emergencies.*

_____ 13. *Obtain costume plots and make-up designs.*

_____ 14. *Invite staff and crews to run-throughs and begin timing scenes.*

_____ 15. *Organize and run the dress parade.*

_____ 16. *Post program information for proofreading and pass on corrections.*

_____ 17. *List and procure additional props.*

_____ 18. *Request make-up designs and time estimates.*

_____ 19. *Follow up on rehearsal notes which require response.*

Harcourt Brace & Company

TECHNICAL REHEARSALS CHECKLIST

Play _____

SM _____

_____ 1. *Post the crew call and assist with the load-in.*

_____ 2. *Arrange the scene dock and prop tables and plan scene shifts.*

_____ 3. *Assign a backstage space for quick changes.*

_____ 4. *Assign, check, and maintain dressing rooms.*

_____ 5. *Set up the communication system for cueing.*

_____ 6. *Attend the paper tech; note and number all cues.*

_____ 7. *List preshow activities including technical equipment checks.*

_____ 8. *Set up backstage lights and spotting lights.*

_____ 9. *Rehearse scenery and prop shifts.*

_____ 10. *Run a dry tech to rehearse calling the show without actors.*

_____ 11. *Run a cue-to-cue to integrate actors' cues with technical effects.*

_____ 12. *Run full technical rehearsals (complete run-throughs with tech).*

_____ 13. *Run the final dress rehearsal exactly like a performance.*

_____ 14. *Assign an ASM to collect and secure actors' valuables.*

_____ 15. *Make a complimentary tickets list and turn it in to the box office manager.*

_____ 16. *Fill out the stage manager's report.*

_____ 17. *Post and follow up on repair sheets and give technical and acting notes.*

_____ 18. *Teach the ASMs to call the show.*

_____ 19. _____

Harcourt Brace & Company

PERFORMANCE CHECKLIST

Play _____

SM _____

_____ 1.   *Arrive early and check stage and house for performance readiness.*

_____ 2.   *Synchronize watches with the house manager.*

_____ 3.   *Call for a lighting, sound, and cueing equipment check.*

_____ 4.   *Check onstage and backstage scenery and props.*

_____ 5.   *Keep visitors out of the booth and backstage areas.*

_____ 6.   *Telephone late actors and crew and replace absent actors.*

_____ 7.   *Give warning calls to actors and crews.*

_____ 8.   *Coordinate curtain time and intermission(s) with the house manager.*

_____ 9.   *Call the show.*

_____ 10. *Supervise scene shifts.*

_____ 11. *Walk the closing of the curtain.*

_____ 12. *Complete the SM report and set up for the next performance.*

_____ 13. *Give acting and crew notes.*

_____ 14. *Maintain the scenery, props, and costumes.*

_____ 15. *Prepare for and run the photo call.*

_____ 16. *Maintain the cast and crew morale.*

_____ 17. *Call and run brush-up rehearsals as needed.*

_____ 18. *Schedule and assist with videotaping the production.*

_____ 19. _____

Harcourt Brace & Company

POSTPRODUCTION
CHECKLIST

Play _____

SM _____

_____ 1. Post strike information.

_____ 2. Participate in the strike.

_____ 3. Return keys and complete all paperwork.

_____ 4. Prepare the production book for your portfolio or the company archives.

_____ 5. Send thank-you letters.

_____ 6. Request letters of recommendation.

_____ 7. Update your resumé.

_____ 8. _____

_____ 9. _____

_____ 10. _____

_____ 11. _____

_____ 12. _____

_____ 13. _____

_____ 14. _____

_____ 15. _____

_____ 16. _____

_____ 17. _____

_____ 18. _____

_____ 19. _____

Harcourt Brace & Company

3

THE PRODUCTION BOOK: FORMAT AND FORMS

The **production book** houses the stage manager's script. It also contains all blocking, cueing, and management information pertaining to the rehearsals and performances of the play. It is sometimes called the *promptbook* or the *production bible.*

With today's video technology, the visuals and sounds of a play may be recorded for posterity. However, the process which created and maintained the product can be viewed only through accurate and legible record keeping, which is the responsibility of the stage manager.

The AEA production contract, in listing the minimal duties of the stage manager, defines the production book as follows:

> 2. He shall assemble and maintain the Prompt Book, which is defined as the accurate playing text and stage business, together with such cue sheets, plots, daily records, etc. as are necessary for the actual technical and artistic operation of the production.

FORMAT

Some stage managers make two production books: one for rehearsals that includes all managerial and organizational forms and notes, interpretative notes, and blocking notes; and one for calling the show that includes all technical cues, warnings for actors, entrance cues, and other blocking notes that cue technical crews. The reason for the second book is to keep technical cues easy to read on an uncluttered page.

I don't have a separate sheet for calling cues. They go into my production book. Why? The book is in my mind. Blocking is often a part of cues–lighting

A stage manager's desk needs to be organized and comfortable. The most important item is the production book, but also notice the computer, desk lamp, cork board for messages and reminders, and other accessories. (Photo by J. B. Alston)

---

designers usually tie light cues to movement—probably because they are less familiar with the lines but also because movement is often the cue.

—CAROL CLARK, AEA STAGE MANAGER

Most stage managers (for lack of time) work with one production book, sometimes removing and filing all materials not necessary to the running of the show when technical rehearsals begin. The *notation format* (see Chapter 4, p. 122) is a form on which the script is typed or copied. It also provides separate spaces for **blocking notations** and for technical cues, thus allowing one production book to serve for both rehearsals and performances.

SELECTION OF BOOK

A loose-leaf binder which holds 8 1/2-by-11-inch paper is standard. For a one-act or short play, a binder with a spine of 1-inch or 1 1/2-inches is adequate to hold the materials collected for that production. For a full-length play, a 2- or 3-inch spine is usually necessary. Additionally, the binder should be hard rather than soft to provide a stable surface for writing. A musical may double the amount of paperwork and necessitate the use of two books: one to hold all rehearsal and performance information, the other to hold all additional management and organizational forms and notes.

DIVIDERS AND CATEGORIES

Forms and notes will begin accumulating as soon as the production process begins. It is important to organize these materials for easy access. Dividers with tabs is the obvious solution. Just as different individuals have different thought processes, so do they have differing methods for organizing. You may wish to organize your records chronologically or departmentally.

SAMPLE: CHRONOLOGICAL ORGANIZATION

1. preaudition notes and forms
2. audition
3. prerehearsal
4. script
5. rehearsal
6. technical
7. performances
8. post performances

SAMPLE: DEPARTMENTAL ORGANIZATION

1. management notes and forms
2. script
3. director
4. actors
5. props
6. scenery
7. costumes and make-up
8. lights and sound

FORMS

Predesigned forms save time, thought, and miscommunications. However, each script, production, theatre, and director is unique, having requirements that must be addressed individually, thereby defying standardization. For this reason, some stage managers prefer to design their own forms for each production. This is a time-consuming trial-and-error project, especially for beginning stage managers. The alternative is to use predesigned forms and edit them, if necessary, to suit your production's needs.

Many theatre production forms, covering every aspect of theatre imaginable, are available both in texts and on computer software. However, most of those forms are created for professional rather than educational or community theatre.

PERSONALIZING AND EDITING FORMS

Personalizing and editing predesigned forms may be accomplished by using correction fluid for subtractions and typing or using simple paste-up techniques for additions. An alternative is to use these forms as guides and generate new ones on a computer.

Your company's graphic identity may be added to each form by covering the existing logo with your company's logo and adding your company's name and address (see Figure 3-1). Your logo may need to be reduced to fit the space allowed.

A form may have a column or division which is unnecessary for your production. Eliminate the column title with correction fluid and type or paste a needed column title over it. If you need additional columns, you may

FIGURE 3.1

AUDITION
NOTES/SCHEDULE

AFRICAN-AMERICAN
DANCE
ENSEMBLE

No. ___ of ___

Date _____

Play _____

By _____

Date/time	Name	Notes

FIGURE 3.2

AUDITION
NOTES/SCHEDULE

Department of Dramatic Art
North Carolina Central University

No. ___ of ___

Date _____

Play _____

By _____

Date/time	Name	Call back?	Role(s) being considered for

subdivide existing columns or use a second page with new column headings covering the original ones (see Figure 3-2).

USING FORMS

How is your handwriting? If it is not decipherable, you are handicapped. You are forced to use a computer or typewriter to generate all written communications. Not all stage managers can afford a laptop computer and printer to use during and between rehearsals, and not all would choose to use one.

> *Frank Hartenstein, stage manager for* Tommy, *uses a computer during rehearsals. He does ground plans on the computer to show the arrangement of scenery during every scene.*
>
> —CAROL CLARK, AEA STAGE MANAGER

A typewriter, though more affordable, is less flexible and (by itself) insufficient. Both of these tools are useful and as a stage manager, you should develop your keyboard skills and become comfortable with a good word-processing program. However, slavery to electronics is not necessary. Minimal practice of simple block lettering will improve your handwriting legibility and the look of your call board, as well as provide some creative release. For exercises to improve your hand lettering, refer to Appendix B.

PRODUCTION FORMS, INSTRUCTIONS, AND SAMPLES

The following pages include forty forms with instructions for and samples of their use. They were designed to allow for individualization and are presented in the order in which they would typically be used.

PREPRODUCTION

 1. Checklist
 2. Blank Form
 3. Script Record
 4. Theatre Information Sheets
 5. Production Fact Sheet
 6. Production Meeting
 7. Program Information Approval
 8. Audition Form

AUDITIONS

 9. Audition Notes/Schedule
10. Cast List

PREREHEARSALS

11. Calendar Six Weeks
12. Calendar Week
13. Contact Sheet
14. Script Breakdown
15. Character Breakdown
16. Prop Breakdown
17. Rehearsal Prop Request
18. Rehearsal Costume Request
19. Publicity Sheet
20. Rehearsal Call

REHEARSALS

21. Sign-in Sheet
22. Production Log
23. Program Acknowledgments
24. Dance Sheet
25. Combat Sheet
26. Accident Report

BLOCKING AND REFINING REHEARSALS

27. Borrowed Items Record
28. Rented Items Record

TECHNICAL REHEARSALS

29. Preset Plot
30. Shift Plot
31. Prop Sheet
32. Costume Change Plot
33. Light Cue Sheet
34. Follow Spot Cue Sheet
35. Sound Cue Sheet
36. Cue Sheet
37. Dimmer/Instrument Check
38. Stage Manager's Report
39. Repair Sheet

PERFORMANCE

40. Photo List

INSTRUCTIONS FOR USING FORMS

Some of the following forms are easily used and do not require instructions. Others benefit from both instructions and samples. When they are reproduced, the forms should be enlarged 142% to fit a standard notebook (8 1/2" × 11").

PREPRODUCTION

The *checklist* is a generic form for anything from a shopping list for props to a preshow list of activities. Use the box on the left to ✓ or X when the purchase or activity is completed.

The *script record* is used to identify who has which script. Each script should be numbered on the front. If a script is found backstage, it is easy to return it to the proper person. It also allows you to keep up with scripts that are borrowed before auditions (if company policy permits loaning scripts). The "return date" column states when the script was returned, releasing the borrower from responsibility.

Some companies expect the script to be returned at the end of the production. Be sure this is clear to the cast when the scripts are assigned.

The *theatre information sheets* provide facts and data necessary for loading-in and running a show. This information is vital for a show which is being toured to an unfamiliar theatre, and it is also important to the designer and technical director when a set has to be moved from a distant **shop** to the stage. The theatre information sheet contains contact information for personnel who can answer additional questions or clarify answers. This form should be filled out by the theatre manager or technical director for that performance space. Copies of the completed form should go to the designer, the technical director, and into the production book.

Ask only for information that is needed, unless you want to place the form in a file for future use of the performance space. Remember, information will change. Curtains may be replaced or discarded; technical equipment may be replaced and updated, and so on. It is wise to get a new information sheet each time a theatre is visited, or to ask for an update on any changes that have taken place since your last visit.

Some theatres have an information sheet or packet already prepared which may be more thorough than the form in this text. Some packets may include information about the stage and equipment but not include information about the loading dock (or lack of one) and other openings through which the scenery must pass.

Do not assume that anything will be available at the site if it is not listed. You may need to request prop tables, ladders, and so on. Check to see that those items listed are actually available, because preplanning is of limited value if your information is incomplete or inaccurate.

The *production fact sheet* contains the basic information needed to become familiar with a production. It should be posted on the callboard and may be copied for each staff, cast, and crew member.

The *production meeting form* has defined spaces for the agenda and for each department in the production. As every production is unique, these divisions may not be appropriate in size or title. Edit them to meet current production and staff needs.

The *program information approval form* should be typed for absolute clarity and to assist in identifying any errors in spelling. Each staff or company member whose name appears on the program should initial or ✓ the box to the left as a confirmation of the accuracy of their name and title. The director or publicist can approve the spelling of the script information. Also, sometimes the department head or crew chief can approve the crew names.

The *audition form* is to be filled out by the actor. It may need editing if the director is looking for specific skills or experience that are not addressed in the form. Your company may have its own audition form. Review and edit it for current production requirements.

Bring paper clips to attach resumés and photographs to the audition form. Be sure the actor's name is on the photograph. The audition form will be your source of information for filling out the contact sheet, therefore it must be complete. After the show is cast, keep all audition forms in a file for future reference.

FIGURE 3.3		SAMPLE SCHEDULE

Schedule: Cross out hours in class or at work.

Time	Sun.	Mon.	Tue.	Wed.	Thur.	Fri.	Sat.	Any additional commitments? Be specific:
9:00			9:30		9:30			
10:00		✕	✕	✕	✕	✕	✱	OCT. 17—WEDDING (BROTHER)
11:00								NOV. 1—GRE (EXAM)
Noon						LAB	WORK	8:00am—12:00 NOON
1:00	✱	✕	✕	✕	✕			
2:00	WORK	✕	1:30	✕	1:30			*I CAN RESCHEDULE WORK
3:00								HOURS AROUND WEEKEND
4:00	4:30						4:30	REHEARSALS
5:00								
6:00								
7:00		CLASS						
8:00								
9:00		9:30						
10:00								

The greatest opportunity for confusion is in filling out the "schedule." If an actor has a commitment which ends on the half-hour, he/she should draw a horizontal line through the middle of the hour block (see Figure 3-3). It may help to post a sample of a completed schedule and to announce the importance of honesty in listing regular rehearsal conflicts and special commitments.

AUDITIONS

The *audition notes/schedule* can be used to list dates and times for interview auditions or to give a time sequence for actors in an open audition. The director will use the form to make comments unless she/he prefers to make notes on the back of the audition form where there will be more space. The director may ask you to take notes dictated during or following each audition. The notes may include no more than whether the actor will be called back and/or the role for which the actor is being considered.

The *cast list* is self-explanatory. However, you might want to add a note above the list, asking all actors to initial beside their name to indicate acceptance of the role.

PREREHEARSALS

The *calendar six weeks* can be used for most productions' rehearsal schedules. There may be planned breaks in rehearsals for holidays, other productions, and so on. If the show requires a longer rehearsal time, you can add weeks to the calendar, making it fit an 8-1/2-by-14-inch format. You can also enlarge the whole form to fill an 11-by-17-inch format in order to make the spaces accommodate more information. The box in the upper left of each space is for writing in the date.

The *calendar week* can be used as a personal or production appointment form. You can post one on the callboard each week with all rehearsals and appointments for production meetings, costume fittings, photo shoots, and so on. This form can also be used for filling out individual schedules.

The *contact sheet* provides everyone's mailing address, phone number, and the hours when they are most accessible. These are times when the individual is not at work, in class, or in rehearsal. With this information, messages can be communicated and appointments and special rehearsals can be scheduled.

The *script breakdown* is used to divide the play into French scenes or beats in order to plan rehearsals (see Figure 3-4). It is also useful to the director for script analysis. French scenes are based on the changing of characters on stage. Each time a character enters or exits the stage, a new scene begins. In a script like *Waiting for Godot,* in which two characters are on stage for the entire play and are briefly visited by other characters on only two occasions, French scenes would not provide enough divisions. Most directors today prefer to divide the script into beats in which a new scene begins whenever the dialogue, mood, or action changes.

The *character breakdown* should use the same divisions as the script breakdown. List all characters in the play and check (✓) those scenes in which each appears (see Figure 3-5). If there are more than twenty scenes, subdivide columns and renumber them.

The *prop breakdown* is simply a prop list which also determines the type of prop, how it is to be found, and any description necessary. Hand props are those props which an actor handles such as a bouquet of flowers, a cane, or a book. Set props are movable units of scenery such as furniture, a tree stump, or a light post. Dress props are items that "dress-up" the scenery such as curtains on a window, books on a shelf, or a mirror on a wall. In listing the props, include any description that the director or designer requests such as color, style, size, and so on.

FIGURE 3.4	SAMPLE SCRIPT BREAKDOWN

SCRIPT BREAKDOWN

No. __1__ of __1__
January 12, 1996
Date
The City Without Love
Play
Kamora Avent, SM
By

Act/Scene	Pages	Characters	Setting/Action
I 1	1–3	Comm., Guard, Anna	street—Anna chided for laughing
2	3–6	Swallow, Anna, Hollow Man	same—song & dance
			stone throwing
3	7–11	Comm., Anna, Soldiers, Swallow, Guard	Guard talks of pity,
		Clown, Urchin	Clown heals Swallow,
			Urchin introduced
4	11–14	Clown, Guard, Anna	Talk about city's coldness

The *rehearsal props request* is a list of props needed during rehearsals (not the final props which will be used in the performance). If a prop needs to be a particular size or might be a safety hazard (such as a table on which an actress must dance), provide that information in the "description" column.

The *rehearsal costumes request* is a list of garments which can substitute for the final costumes. They are usually requested because the actors need to adjust to the style (such as a hoop skirt), the restrictions (such as a monk's robe), or to help the actors get into character. Also, if an actor must fight in a cape, mask, or other costume piece which might affect movement, be sure to get a rehearsal garment of the same type so there will be little adjustment when dress rehearsals begin.

The *publicity sheet* is to be filled out by the individual it represents. Ask that it be typed or printed in block letters. Also ask that experience be listed chronologically, beginning with earliest and ending with most recent.

The *rehearsal call* form can be used to schedule simultaneous rehearsals (such as dance, voice, and acting); to schedule rehearsals for several plays (such as a series of one-acts); to schedule individual scene work throughout

FIGURE 3.5	SAMPLE CHARACTER BREAKDOWN

CHARACTER BREAKDOWN

No. __1__ of __1__

January 12, 1996
Date
THE CITY WITHOUT LOVE
Play
Kamora Avent, SM
By

Scenes

Character	1	2	3	4	5	6	7	8	9	10	11	12	13	14	15	16	17	18	19	20
Commentator	x		x		x		x			x			x				x			
Clown			x	x	x	x	x			x			x	x	x		x			
Mayor				x		x		x	x	x	x	x	x			x				
Anna	x	x	x	x			x			x		x		x	x		x			
Hollow Man		x			x		x		x	x	x	x	x	x			x			
Swallow		x	x										x		x		x			

the day; or to give call times and scenes for a full week of rehearsals (see Figure 3-6). If it is used for one rehearsal in one rehearsal space, you might replace the word "place" with "characters" to remind the actors of their scenes.

REHEARSALS

The *sign-in sheet* should include the names of cast members and rehearsal crews. Each sheet represents one week of the rehearsal period. You may have them initial beside their name or you may have an ASM hold the sheet in a clip board and check each name off as they arrive. When it is time for rehearsal to begin, put a diagonal line in the upper left box of those actors who have been called but have not yet arrived. If they do not show up at all, put an "x" in the box.

The *production log* is the rehearsal diary and should be filled out each night with any information important to the rehearsal or to the production. It may include memos for the director or other staff members or notes to yourself about things to do the next day or after rehearsal. Rename department blocks if those listed are inappropriate. As the production log will be a permanent part of the production book, do not use it for personal information.

FIGURE 3.6	SAMPLE REHEARSAL CALL

 REHEARSAL CALL

I'M NOT RAPPAPORT
Play

OCT. 16–21   BARRY WILDER
Date   *Stage Manager*

Scenes		Place	Time
OCT. 16 SCENES 5–9		THEATRE	7:00 pm
OCT. 17 ACT I		THEATRE	7:00 pm
OCT. 18 ACT II	MIDGE —— RM 105 THEATRE		3:15 pm 7:30 pm
OCT. 19 RUN-THROUGH	NAT —— RM 105 THEATRE		4:00 pm 8:00 pm
OCT. 20 RUN-THROUGH		THEATRE	7:00 pm

OCT. 21
    NO REHEARSAL
    PHOTO SESSION—EVERYONE
		THEATRE	1:00 pm

The *program acknowledgments* form serves two purposes. It provides information for the program and it becomes an address list for thank-you notes following the production.

The *dance sheet* is for the choreographer, the costumer, and for you. The "phone" column is for scheduling special rehearsals or costume fittings or for calling late dancers.

The *combat sheet,* like the dance sheet, is for the fight director, the costumer, and you. It is a reminder of the equipment needed for safe fight rehearsals and any other notes which might aid in reducing the potential danger of these rehearsals.

The *accident report* is important in documenting the details of an accident or injury and the care that was provided.

BLOCKING AND REFINING REHEARSALS

The *borrowed items record* and the *rented items record* are forms for the ASM in charge of props. Get a copy for the production book.

TECHNICAL REHEARSALS

The *preset plot* is the plan for the placement of properties which are on stage at the beginning of Act 1 and following an intermission (see Figure 3-7). After the last curtain call, the stage is usually set up for the next performance. This form is for the ASM in charge of properties, and a copy should be kept in the production book.

The *shift plot* is the plan for the moving of properties and scenery during an act (usually done in a blackout or under dimmed lights). This form is also for the ASM in charge of the properties running crew and for your production book (see Figure 3-8).

The *prop sheet* is a list to be filled out by the ASM in charge of props and posted on stage left and/or stage right, beside the prop table. It should include all the properties that will be carried on stage by an actor or crew member from that side of the stage (see Figure 3-9).

The *costume change plot* is for planning quick changes. Most quick changes are done backstage or on stage during a blackout. There should be a specific location at which the changes will occur. The costume change plot should be posted near it so the dresser can have the garments ready (see Figure 3-10).

The *light cue sheet* is for the board operator to note lighting cues. Be sure the cue numbers correlate with the master cue list in the production book.

The *follow spot cue sheet* is for the operator of the **follow spot.** Be sure the cue numbers correlate with the master cue list in the production book.

The *sound cue sheet* is for the sound technician. However, sound effects may come from various sources and locations. Edit the form to suit the equipment and production.

The *cue sheet* is a generic form which can be used by any technician or for the stage manager's master list (see Figure 3-11).

The *dimmer/instrument check* lists all of the lighting instruments used in the production, their dimmers, where they are located, and their area of **focus.** It is used by the lighting board operator and stage manager to check the operating status of the dimmers and instruments and the accuracy of focus.

The *stage manager's report* is a form to be filled out after each technical rehearsal and performance (see Figure 3-12). The house manager checks the times listed, gives the house count (number in audience), and signs the form. The stage manager also signs the form and gives a copy to the director or other supervising personnel.

FIGURE 3.7	SAMPLE PRESET PLOT

PRESET PLOT

No. <u>1</u>   of <u>1</u>

<u>APRIL 10, 1990</u>
Date
<u>MOTHER HICKS</u>
Play
<u>ASM</u>
For

ACT II — CABIN

Item	When	Where	Description/Instructions	Set by
COOK FIRE		Center	FROM STAGE L	BARRY
RABBIT BOX		UR	FROM STAGE R	SUE
PALLET		¿8 L	FROM STAGE L	BARRY
POT		OVER FIRE	FROM STAGE L	BARRY
GLASS		R OF FIRE	FROM STAGE R	SUE
CHAIR 1		UL	FROM STAGE L	BARRY
CHAIR 2		R	FROM STAGE R	SUE
CART		6	FROM STAGE R	JOHN

Notes

Ground plan

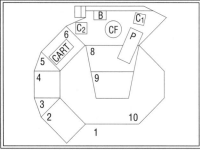

FIGURE 3.8	SAMPLE SHIFT PLOT

SHIFT PLOT

No. __1__ of __1__

APRIL 11, 1990
Date
MOTHER HICKS
Play
ASM — RIGHT
By

Item	Cue	Entrance	Shift instructions	Exit	Shift by
CART	BLACKOUT	UL	ROLL OUT	DL	JOHN
BARREL	LTS. DIM IN	DL	ROLL IN	DR	BARRY
COUNTER	"	UL	LOCK WHEELS	DR	JOHN & SUE
REGISTER	"	DR	ON COUNTER	DL	BARRY
CRATES	"	DR	STACK BARREL	DL	JOHN
JARS	"	DL	ON COUNTER	DR	BARRY
CHAIR	"	DR	BESIDE BARREL	DL	SUE

Shift diagram

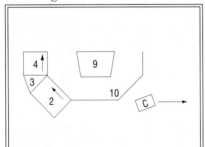
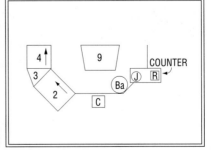

FIGURE 3.9	SAMPLE PROP SHEET

PROP SHEET

No. __1__ of __2__
APRIL 10, 1990
Date
MOTHER HICKS
Play
ASM
By

Stage left ☐ Stage right ☑ Running crew: JOHN, SUE, BARRY

No.	Item	Starting position	Ending position	Notes
1	CART	R	L	ACTOR – CREW
2	CRATES	R	R	CREW
3	REGISTER	R TABLE	R TABLE	CREW
4	NEWSPAPER	R TABLE	L TABLE	ACTOR

FIGURE 3.10	SAMPLE COSTUME CHANGE PLOT

COSTUME CHANGE PLOT

No. __1__ of __1__
NOV. 12, 1995
Date
RAPPAPORT
Play
BARRY WILDER
By

No.	Character	Dresser	When	Where	Off	On	Time
1	MITCH	JAN	SC 2	R	JACKET	SWEATER	30 sec.
2	NAT	DON	SC 2	L	COAT, TIE SLACKS	GREY SUIT & TIE	45 sec.

FIGURE 3.11	SAMPLE CUE SHEET

CUE SHEET

FLY DECK

No. _____ of _____
Date
APRIL 4
Play
CITY WITHOUT LOVE
By
ALICE SMITH

Cue#	Page	Act/Scene	Cue (line, action)	Count	Instructions/Description
1	31	I 10	END OF MAYOR'S SONG	6	28 IN
2	34	I 11	"I HEAR FOOTSTEPS"	6	28 OUT 16 IN
3	42	II 13	HOLLOW MAN EXITS	6	16 OUT
4	52	II 16	CLOWN EXITS	6	16 IN

FIGURE 3.12	SAMPLE STAGE MANAGER'S REPORT

Performance Time Log

	Act I	Intermission	Act II	Intermission	Act III	Total time
	slated: 8:15 actual: 8:20 down: 9:00 TOTAL: 40 min.	slated: 10 min. actual: 10 min.	up: 9:10 down: 10:00 TOTAL: 50 min.	slated: actual: ✕	up: down: ✕ TOTAL:	1hr. 40min.
delays	AUD. BEING SEATED	none	none			

The *repair sheet* is to be posted in each dressing room (for costumes) and backstage (for props, scenery, or equipment). The form can be filled out by each person reporting a repair need. Assign an ASM to follow up on getting the repairs done, or do it yourself.

PERFORMANCES

The *photo list* includes all requested production photographs. The director and each designer will want photos and should have an opportunity for input. Have each one fill out a photo list, then make a master list following a backwards chronological order. Since the shoot usually takes place after a performance, you can begin with the costumes used at the end of the show and work your way forward.

No. _____ of _____

CHECKLIST

Date _____

Play _____

For _____

☐ _____   ☐ _____
☐ _____   ☐ _____
☐ _____   ☐ _____
☐ _____   ☐ _____
☐ _____   ☐ _____
☐ _____   ☐ _____
☐ _____   ☐ _____
☐ _____   ☐ _____
☐ _____   ☐ _____
☐ _____   ☐ _____
☐ _____   ☐ _____
☐ _____   ☐ _____
☐ _____   ☐ _____
☐ _____   ☐ _____
☐ _____   ☐ _____
☐ _____   ☐ _____
☐ _____   ☐ _____
☐ _____   ☐ _____
☐ _____   ☐ _____
☐ _____   ☐ _____

Harcourt Brace & Company

No. _____ of _____

SCRIPT RECORD

Date _____

Play _____

For _____

Script #	Actor	Return date	Contact information

Harcourt Brace & Company

Date _____

By _____

**THEATRE
INFORMATION 1**

Theatre _____ Phone numbers _____

Address _____   _____

_____ Zip _____ *Fax number* _____

Contact for theatre information:

Name _____ *Phone number* _____

House

Seating capacity _____ *Orchestra* _____ *Mezzanine* _____ *Balcony* _____

Stage

Proscenium _____ *Thrust* _____ *Arena* _____ *Other* _____

Floor: flat _____ *raked* _____ *surface* _____ *condition* _____

Can screws be used in floor? _____ *Can floor be painted?* _____

Measurements: proscenium opening (width) _____ *(height)* _____

apron to curtain line _____ *apron to back wall* _____

apron width _____ *shape of apron* _____

Traps: number _____ *location* _____

Rigging

Type (fly) _____ *(dead hung)* _____ *Location of rail* _____

Number of lines available for use _____ *Length of battens* _____

Location (from curtain line) _____

Maximum weight per batten _____ *Maximum height of drops/scenery* _____

Number of electrics _____ *Location (from curtain line)* _____

Harcourt Brace & Company

THEATRE
INFORMATION 2

Date _____

By _____

Curtains

Type	#	Width	Height	Color	Location	Rigid?	Moveable?
cyc							
scrim							
grand dr.							
travellers							
borders							
legs							

Load-in access

Location _____ Distance to stage _____

Outside door: width _____ height _____ height from ground _____

Smallest opening that must be used for load-in: width _____ height _____

Harcourt Brace & Company

PRODUCTION
FACT SHEET

Date _____

By _____

Play _____

Company _____ Type of contract _____

Scripts available from _____

Producer _____ Playwright _____

Composer _____ Lyricist _____

Auditions (dates) _____ (times) _____

     (place) _____

Rehearsals (dates) _____ (place) _____

Technical rehearsals (dates) _____

Performances (dates) _____ (theatre) _____

Management staff: _____

_____

Directing staff: _____

_____

Design staff: _____

_____

SM staff: _____

_____

Technical staff: _____

_____

Harcourt Brace & Company

No. _____ of _____

**PRODUCTION
MEETING**

Date/Time _____

Play _____

By _____

Presiding: _____ Position: _____

Staff present: _____

_____

Agenda:

_____   _____

_____   _____

_____   _____

_____   _____

Notes:

Director and stage manager	Set and lights	Props

Costumes and make-up	Sound and music	Management and miscellaneous

Harcourt Brace & Company

No. _____ of _____

PROGRAM
INFORMATION
APPROVAL

Date _____

Play _____

By _____

☐ **Production** _____

☐ *Playwright(s)* _____

☐ *Composer* _____ ☐ *Lyricist* _____

☐ *Producer(s)* _____

☐ *Artistic Dir.* _____ ☐ *Theatre Mgr.* _____

☐ *Bus. Mgr.* _____ ☐ *Publicist* _____

☐ *House Mgr.* _____ ☐ *Box Office* _____

☐ *Director* _____ ☐ *Assistant* _____

☐ *Prod. SM* _____ ☐ *Stage Mgr.* _____

☐ *Asst. SM* _____ ☐ *Prod. Asst.* _____

☐ *Choreo.* _____ ☐ *Dance Capt.* _____

☐ *Fight Dir.* _____ ☐ *Fight Capt.* _____

☐ *Music Dir.* _____ ☐ *Assistant* _____

☐ *Choral Dir.* _____ ☐ *Assistant* _____

☐ *Scene Des.* _____ ☐ *Assistant* _____

☐ *Lt. Des.* _____ ☐ *Electrician* _____

☐ *Sound Des.* _____ ☐ *Sound Tech.* _____

☐ *Prop Des.* _____ ☐ *Prop Mas./Mis.* _____

☐ *Cos. Des.* _____ ☐ *Assistant* _____

Harcourt Brace & Company

No. _____ of _____

PROGRAM
INFORMATION
APPROVAL
(continued)

_____

Date

_____

Play

_____

By

☐ *Make-up Des.* _____ ☐ *Hair* _____

☐ *Tech. Dir.* _____ ☐ *Master Carp.* _____

☐ *Const. Crew* _____

_____

☐ *Paint Crew* _____

☐ *Light Crew* _____

☐ *Sound Crew* _____

☐ *Prop Crew* _____

☐ *Makeup Crew* _____

☐ *Costume Crew* _____

☐ *Dressers* _____

☐ *Photographer* _____

☐ *Graphic Des.* _____

☐ *Production Secretary* _____

☐ *Other* _____

☐ *Notes:* _____

_____

_____

_____

Harcourt Brace & Company

AUDITION
FORM

Date _____

Play _____

Name _____ Phone _____

Address _____

Student: yes ☐ no ☐ if yes, school _____

Employed: yes ☐ no ☐ if yes, where _____

Union affiliation _____ Agent/Agency _____

Schedule: Cross out hours in class or at work.

Time	Sun.	Mon.	Tue.	Wed.	Thur.	Fri.	Sat.
9:00							
10:00							
11:00							
Noon							
1:00							
2:00							
3:00							
4:00							
5:00							
6:00							
7:00							
8:00							
9:00							
10:00							

Any additional
commitments? Be specific:

_____
_____
_____
_____
_____
_____
_____

Harcourt Brace & Company

AUDITION FORM
(continued)

Date _____

Play _____

Role(s) auditioning for: _____

Height _____ *Weight* _____ *Age range* _____ *Hair color* _____ *Eye color* _____

Vocal quality _____ *Vocal range* _____ *Solo* _____ *Chorus* _____

Dance: tap ☐ *ballet* ☐ *jazz* ☐ *other* _____ *Play instrument* _____

Stage combat: (specify) _____ *Other specialties* _____

Physical fitness: (any relevant problems) _____

Acting experience: Attach resumé or list roles, plays, dates, theatres (continue on back).

_____

_____

_____

_____

_____

_____

_____

_____

_____

_____

Harcourt Brace & Company

No. _____ of _____

AUDITION NOTES/SCHEDULE

Date _____

Play _____

By _____

Date/Time	Name	Notes

Harcourt Brace & Company

No. _____ of _____

CAST LIST

Date _____

Play _____

Director _____

Stage manager _____

Character	Actor	Initials	Understudy	Initials

Harcourt Brace & Company

CALENDAR
SIX WEEKS

No. _____ of _____

Date _____

Play _____

For _____

Sunday	Monday	Tuesday	Wednesday	Thursday	Friday	Saturday

Harcourt Brace & Company

No. _____ of _____

Date _____

CALENDAR
WEEK

Play _____

For _____

Time	Sunday	Monday	Tuesday	Wednesday	Thursday	Friday	Saturday
8:00							
9:00							
10:00							
11:00							
12:00							
1:00							
2:00							
3:00							
4:00							
5:00							
6:00							
7:00							
8:00							
9:00							
10:00							

Harcourt Brace & Company

CONTACT SHEET

No. _____ of _____

Date _____

Play _____

Stage manager _____

Cast/Crew/Staff	Address	Phone	Hours available

Harcourt Brace & Company

No. _____ of _____

Date _____

SCRIPT BREAKDOWN

Play _____

By _____

Act/Scene	Pages	Characters	Setting/Action

Harcourt Brace & Company

No. _____ of _____

**CHARACTER
BREAKDOWN**

Date _____

Play _____

By _____

Scenes

Character	1	2	3	4	5	6	7	8	9	10	11	12	13	14	15	16	17	18	19	20

Harcourt Brace & Company

			No. _____ of _____

PROP BREAKDOWN

Date _____

Play _____

By _____

Hand	Set	Dress	Designer: _____ Stage manager: _____ Description: _____	Stock	Borrow	Rent	Buy	Build

Harcourt Brace & Company

**REHEARSAL
PROPS REQUEST**

No. _____ of _____

Date _____

Play _____

By _____

To: _____

Prop	Description	Hand	Set	Dress

Harcourt Brace & Company

No. _____ of _____

REHEARSAL COSTUMES REQUEST

Date _____

Play _____

By _____

To: _____

Costume piece	Character/Actor	Size/Measurements	Date needed

Harcourt Brace & Company

PUBLICITY SHEET

Date _____

Play _____

Name (as you wish it on all publicity) _____

Position/Role/Crew _____

Education: highest degree _____ from _____

If currently in school: classification _____ major _____

          name and address of school _____

Honors/Awards _____

_____

Union affiliations _____

Parents: name _____

          address _____

          hometown newspaper _____

Theatre and other performance experience:
(If list is long, include only most notable and/or most recent experience.)

Play	Role/Position	Date	Theatre

Harcourt Brace & Company

No. _____ of _____

REHEARSAL CALL

_____
Play

_____
Date

_____
Stage manager

Scenes	Place	Time

Harcourt Brace & Company

No. _____ of _____

SIGN-IN SHEET

Week (dates) _____

Play _____

Stage manager _____

☑ Late   ☒ Absent

Name	Sun.	Mon.	Tue.	Wed.	Thur.	Fri.	Sat.

Harcourt Brace & Company

	No. _____ of _____

PRODUCTION LOG

Date _____

Play _____

Stage manager _____

_____

_____

_____

_____

_____

_____

_____

_____

Director	Properties	Costumes/Make-up
Scenery	Lights	Sound

Harcourt Brace & Company

PROGRAM
ACKNOWLEDGMENTS

No. _____ of _____

Date _____

Play _____

By _____

Name	Acknowledged for	Address and phone number

Harcourt Brace & Company

No. _____ of _____

Date _____

DANCE SHEET

Play _____

By _____

Dance title _____

Choreographer _____ Dance captain _____

Music _____

Tape ☐ Live ☐ Musician(s) _____

Dancers	Phone	Notes

Harcourt Brace & Company

No. _____ *of* _____

COMBAT SHEET

Date

Play

By

Fight title _____

Fight director _____ *Fight captain* _____

Music/Sound effects _____

Tape ☐ *Live* ☐ *Musician(s)/Sound technician* _____

Fighters	Phone	Weapons/Equipment	Notes

Harcourt Brace & Company

No. _____ of _____

ACCIDENT REPORT

Date _____

Play _____

By _____

Name of injured person _____ Title _____

Address _____

Phone _____ SS# _____

Name of supervisor _____ Title _____

Account of accident: (time) _____ (date) _____

(location) _____

(description) _____

_____

_____

_____

_____

First aid given: _____

_____

_____

_____

Signature: _____   _____
        (injured person)   *(supervisor)*

_____   _____
        (person filling out form)   *(witness to accident)*

Harcourt Brace & Company

BORROWED
ITEMS
RECORD

No. _____ of _____

Date

Play

By

No.	Item	Borrowed from / Borrowed by	Dates: received	due back	returned

Harcourt Brace & Company

RENTED ITEMS RECORD

No. _____ of _____

Date _____

Play _____

By _____

No.	Item	Rented from / Rented by	Dates: received	due back	returned	Cost

Harcourt Brace & Company

PRESET PLOT

No. _____ of _____

Date _____

Play _____

For _____

Item	When	Where	Description/Instructions	Set by

Notes: _____

_____

_____

_____

_____

Ground plan _____

Harcourt Brace & Company

SHIFT PLOT

No. _____ of _____

Date _____

Play _____

For _____

Item	Cue	Entrance	Shift instructions	Exit	Shift by

Shift diagram

Harcourt Brace & Company

No. _____ of _____

Date _____

PROP SHEET

Play _____

By _____

Stage left ☐   *Stage right* ☐   *Running crew:* _____

No.	Item	Starting position	Ending position	Notes

Harcourt Brace & Company

COSTUME CHANGE
PLOT

No. _____ of _____

Date _____

Play _____

By _____

No.	Character	Dresser	When	Where	Off	On	Time

Harcourt Brace & Company

No. _____ of _____

Date _____

LIGHT
CUE SHEET

Play _____

By _____

Cue no.	Preset	Count	Instructions

Harcourt Brace & Company

No. _____ of _____

Date _____

FOLLOW SPOT
CUE SHEET

Play _____

By _____

Cue no.	Act/Scene	Cue (line, action)	Intensity	Iris	Color	Instructions

Harcourt Brace & Company

No. _____ of _____

**SOUND
CUE SHEET**

Date _____

Play _____

By _____

Cue no.	Count	Deck	Channel levels				Instructions
			1	2	3	4	

Harcourt Brace & Company

No. _____ of _____

CUE SHEET

Date _____

Play _____

By _____

Cue no.	Page	Act/Scene	Cue (line, action)	Count	Instructions/Description

Harcourt Brace & Company

No. _____ of _____

DIMMER/ INSTRUMENT CHECK

Date _____

Play _____

By _____

Dimmer no.	No. of Instruments	Instrument location	Instrument color	Area of focus	Notes

Harcourt Brace & Company

STAGE MANAGER'S REPORT

Date _____

Play _____

Performance time log

Act I	Intermission	Act II	Intermission	Act III	Total time
slated: actual: down: Total:	slated: actual:	up: down: Total:	slated: actual:	up: down: Total:	
delays					

Crew notes

ASM _____

Props _____

Running _____

Costumes _____

Lights _____

Sound _____

(Other) _____

Performance irregularities _____

_____

_____

Comments _____

_____

*House count:*_____ *House manager:*_____ *Stage manager:*_____
                              (sign)   *(sign)*

Harcourt Brace & Company

No. _____ of _____

REPAIR SHEET

Date _____

Play _____

By _____

Costume ☐   Prop ☐   Scenery ☐   Equipment ☐

Name	Date	Item	Description of problem	Done

Harcourt Brace & Company

No. _____ of _____

PHOTO LIST

Date _____

Play _____

By _____

No.	Act/Scene	Characters	Description	Bl/Wh	Color

Harcourt Brace & Company

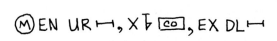 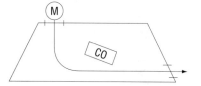

Transcription: Mary enters through the upstage right door, crosses below the
couch, and exits through the downstage left door.

There are some notation conventions used by all stage managers. They have
evolved from common sense, experience, and necessity. The above notations
on the left would be readable for most SMs. The only new symbols in the example above are those for "below" and "door." The stage picture on the right
can be read even more quickly and easily. However, the conventions are few
and notations can become far more complex than those above. The purpose of
this chapter is to take the fear out of first-time blocking rehearsals and to present a system for organizing and making notations that makes it quick and easy
to record and transcribe even complicated movements of multiple characters.

DOCUMENTATION

The stage manager is responsible for documenting all of the director's blocking
and other instructions to the actors as well as noting all technical cues. These
notes are then used to maintain the integrity of the director's concept during
rehearsals and performances. Even if the director preblocks, he/she usually

makes changes during rehearsals and does not have time to record them. Therefore, the SM's notes are usually the only written record of the director's final artistic creation.

SCRIPT NOTATIONS

The SM's notations are made on the master script which is housed in the production book. This is accomplished during blocking rehearsals and can be a traumatizing experience for the first-time stage manager. Traditionally, notes are made in the margin of the script and sometimes on the facing page. Because of the writing speed required to keep up with the director's blocking instructions and because of the number of movements which may occur on a single line of dialogue, the script and notes can become crowded and difficult to read. Technical cues and additional rehearsal notes compete for space and increase the confusion.

NOTATION CLARITY

Most stage managers gradually develop their own way of organizing notes as well as their own shorthand for making note-taking faster. However, they are usually the only interpreters of their notes, and even they may have difficulty reading their own writing or remembering what an abbreviation or a symbol meant several weeks later—or possibly even at the next rehearsal. Some energetic compulsive SMs type all blocking notations after each rehearsal in a second book to avoid any chance of confusion. This is usually a waste of time because blocking usually changes throughout the first weeks and sometimes right up until opening night. Besides your immediate need for well-organized readable notations, there are many additional reasons for keeping an up-to-date, legible production book:

1. An accident or emergency can occur, causing the original SM to leave a production. (No matter how stoic you are, there are times when the show must go on without you.)
2. A show may be revived or regularly restaged (such as an outdoor drama performed every summer or an annual production such as *A Christmas Carol*).
3. A touring company with new actors may have to be blocked and rehearsed by the SM without the help of the director.
4. A long-running show may lose its vitality after time and require brush-up rehearsals or the blocking of replacement actors at regular intervals.

The need is obvious. The solution is a notation system which is tried and proven, is quick and easy to learn, allows for speed both in making and reading notes, and has a key for others to use in reading the production book.

NOTATION SYSTEMS FOR DANCE AND COMBAT

There are several notation systems for dance. All are cumbersome and awkward for theatre. Dance notations are more thorough than those required for blocking actors. A choreographer plans each detail of gesture for a dancer while the director allows much physical character interpretation to come from the actor. This character development grows throughout the rehearsal process and may not be set until the production opens. Consequently, the SM focuses on notating the use of stage space correlated with dialogue and technical cues. There really is not time in a blocking rehearsal to do more. Dance notations for musical plays are discussed in Chapter 6.

Most fight directors develop a personal system for noting armed combat. Several have been published. *Stage Combat: The Action to the Word* by William Hobbs and *Weapons in the Theatre* by Arthur Wise both contain notation systems for armed combat that have been adopted in part or in full by many actor/fighters and fight choreographers. Notations for unarmed combat are discussed in Chapter 5.

SCHNEIDER NOTATION SYSTEM

The Schneider Notation System is the only published system for noting stage movement, unarmed combat, and dance for musical theatre. The system makes the documentation and reading of blocking and technical cues fast, accurate, and consistent. It has evolved through time, use, and input from many educational and professional stage managers, directors, choreographers, and fight directors. First-time stage managers usually use it in its entirety; veteran stage managers usually adopt parts of it to augment the system they have developed for themselves.

> *As a director, the Schneider Notation System is a valuable tool. As a teacher, it is irreplaceable in its ability to interest, motivate, and educate the novice stage manager. I have also seen people who have stage managed in community theatre for years embrace the System and its principles.*
>
> —BRANDON DAUGHTRY, FREELANCE DIRECTOR AND PLAYWRIGHT

> *Every major at Catawba College Theatre Arts is required to study the Schneider Notation System. Whether preparing actors, directors, design/tech, or stage managers, it is the strongest tool yet devised to quickly and accurately record the details necessary to our craft.*
>
> —DAYNA ANDERSON, SCHUFORD SCHOOL OF PERFORMING ARTS,
> CATWABA COLLEGE

The system takes the traditional conventions, symbols, and abbreviations and adds to them a format for organizing script and notations, more symbols, and the forms in Chapter 3.

TRADITIONALLY USED SYMBOLS, ABBREVIATIONS, AND TERMS

Notation conventions adopted by most stage managers, directors, and actors include character names, easily recognized shortening of common words, stage geography, and terms unique to blocking and technical rehearsals.

Character names are represented by a circled initial (see Figure 4-2). If two or more characters have the same initial, give the first two letters of the other characters' names, reserving the single initial for the character whose name is likely to be used most often.

Abbreviations which are easily recognized can be used in place of full words or symbols. The following are samples of commonly used abbreviations:

EN	enter	Dk	dark	Sw	sideways
EX	exit	Lt	light	Pt	point
W	with	Ba	Back	Co	combination (dance)
Wh	while	Fr	front	Stg	stage
Lg	large	Sd	side	Lk	look
Sm	small	Bw	backward		
Gr	group	Fw	forward		

Stage geography is used to identify positions and movements of characters. Whatever the shape or size of the stage, it must be divided into areas in order to verbalize and notate blocking positions and movements (see Figure 4-3). There are three architectural styles for theatrical stages which are commonly used today: (a) **proscenium,** (b) **thrust,** and (c) **arena.** Many universities also have a **black box** theatre, which is basically a large empty room (usually painted black), that can be used for experimental staging, placing the acting area and audience in any shape or position desired.

"Left" and "right" are determined by the actor's left or right as he/she faces the audience. Since the arena stage has seating on all sides and may be square or round, using the traditional divisions and directions will require additional considerations (see Figure 4-4a). Set up the stage manager's desk in

FIGURE 4.2

Ⓢ Schill Ⓢt Stephen

Ⓒ Claire Ⓒh Child

FIGURE 4.3

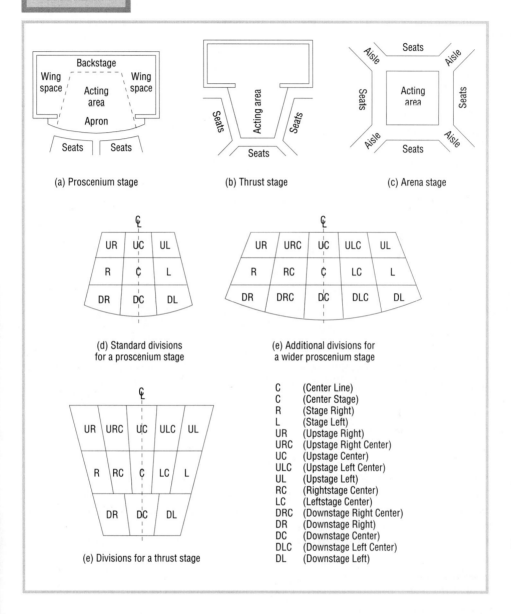

(a) Proscenium stage   (b) Thrust stage   (c) Arena stage

(d) Standard divisions
for a proscenium stage

(e) Additional divisions for
a wider proscenium stage

(e) Divisions for a thrust stage

C   (Center Line)
C   (Center Stage)
R   (Stage Right)
L   (Stage Left)
UR   (Upstage Right)
URC   (Upstage Right Center)
UC   (Upstage Center)
ULC   (Upstage Left Center)
UL   (Upstage Left)
RC   (Rightstage Center)
LC   (Leftstage Center)
DRC   (Downstage Right Center)
DR   (Downstage Right)
DC   (Downstage Center)
DLC   (Downstage Left Center)
DL   (Downstage Left)

the same location for every rehearsal and define that quadrant as the down-stage side. You can also tape the floor into sections, labeling "right," "left," "up-stage," and "downstage" as a reminder for the actors and director.

If the stage is round and more divisions are desired, there are two tech-niques which use familiar terms. The stage may be given geographical labels

FIGURE 4.4

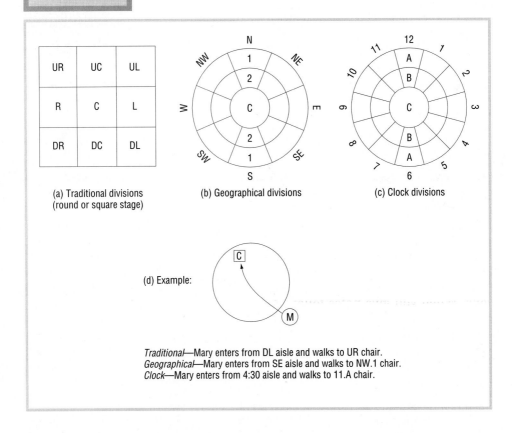

(a) Traditional divisions
(round or square stage)

(b) Geographical divisions

(c) Clock divisions

(d) Example:

Traditional—Mary enters from DL aisle and walks to UR chair.
Geographical—Mary enters from SE aisle and walks to NW.1 chair.
Clock—Mary enters from 4:30 aisle and walks to 11.A chair.

with the stage manager's desk always being located south of the stage (see Figure 4-4b); or the stage may be treated like a clock with the stage manager's desk always being at six o'clock (see Figure 4-4c). For each of these techniques, numbered or alphabetized concentric circles radiating from the center provide more areas.

Terms that are commonly used in blocking and technical rehearsals include the following:

- cross—move or walk
- above—behind, in back of, upstage of
- below—in front of, downstage of
- in—move in the direction of center stage
- out—move in the direction of the wings or offstage
- full front—turn body and face to the audience
- open—turn body or face toward the audience

- profile–turn to face stage left or stage right
- close–turn body or face away from the audience
- full back–turn back to the audience
- fade in–technical term for lights or sound, meaning to slowly increase intensity (lights) or volume (sound)
- fade out–technical term for lights or sound, meaning to slowly decrease intensity (lights) or volume (sound)
- cross fade–slowly fade out one lighted area or sound while simultaneously fading in another lighted area or sound

SCHNEIDER NOTATION SYSTEM

It has been mentioned several times in this text that the SM's primary directive is to maintain the integrity of the director's concept. This means that in the director's absence, the SM must keep the performance and technical aspects of the show consistent. Actors may add stage business or change line interpretation which can affect the tempo, the **focus,** even the meaning of a scene. When you give notes following a performance or when you rehearse an understudy or a replacement, you must not change the director's original intent even if you disagree with it. The only way to keep a long-running show consistent is through accurate and complete documentation, and in order for records to be useful, they must be well organized and legible. The Schneider Notation System will assist you in achieving this goal.

> *I really cannot stress the importance of this enough. In working with different stage managers on collegiate and professional levels, I realize the importance of organization. Organization not only for the individual but for the profession as a whole. I often see people trying to reinvent the theatrical wheel. When you have a method as concise as this System, there is no need for trial and error. The Schneider Notation System is the perfect complement to today's ultra-modern and technically advanced style of theatre.*
>
> —KIMBERLY STRANGE, AEA STAGE MANAGER

The Schneider Notation System includes the following:

1. A graph designed for the purpose of organizing space and making movement notations and technical cues easier to record and interpret;
2. Symbols for recording pacing, intensity, stage pictures, movement, direction, position, gesture, set and dress properties, and technical cues;
3. Forms (presented in Chapter 3) to aid in communication, documentation, and organization.

NOTATION GRAPH

Actors' movements (blocking) must be correlated with dialogue and are therefore noted on or beside the script dialogue. Published scripts are usually small and simply do not have adequate margins for holding all of the notations taken by a stage manager. Several approaches attempt to correct this deficiency.

The traditional method for entering a script into the production book is to cut an opening or window in a sheet of 8-1/2-by-11-inch unlined notebook paper. The window is sized to fit the text of the script page. The script is then glued to the window using rubber cement. The window makes it possible for both sides of the script to be read, and the frame or border surrounding the text is used for making notations. However, this is still an inadequate amount of space for blocking notes, technical cues, and stage pictures.

A second technique is to retype or photocopy the script so that it has dialogue on only one side of the page. This allows the facing page (back of the previous page) to be used for making notes. The space is adequate but lacks organization.

The notation graph for the Schneider Notation System provides columns in the margins of the script and on the facing page (see Figure 4-5). These columns divide notes into pacing, intensity, stage pictures, stage movement, script, and technical cues. Make a copy of the form (see pages 122–123), enlarging it to 142% and use one of the following methods for adding your text:

1.   Cut an opening in the script format which fits the text of the script. Frame the text with the opening of the script format and photocopy it. (If the margins are consistent in size, this is the best method.)

or

2.   Trim the margins around the dialogue to make it as small as possible and then place it on the script column and photocopy the page. (If the margins are irregular in width, this is the best method.)

or

3.   Make multiple copies of the format and then type or photocopy the script onto these pages. (This means copying twice on one side of the paper, but it allows you to bypass the measuring and cutting or trimming process.)

After the entire script is copied, the printed sheets are turned and the other side of the notation graph is copied on the backs of the script pages (see Figure 4-5).

Pacing refers to the tempo or speed of the scene. Symbols used in this column are also used to note the rate of individual character movement and/or delivery of lines (see Figure 4-6).

Most stage managers use this column only when there are definite changes in tempo such as when a scene is building to a **climax,** slowing for suspense,

FIGURE 4.5

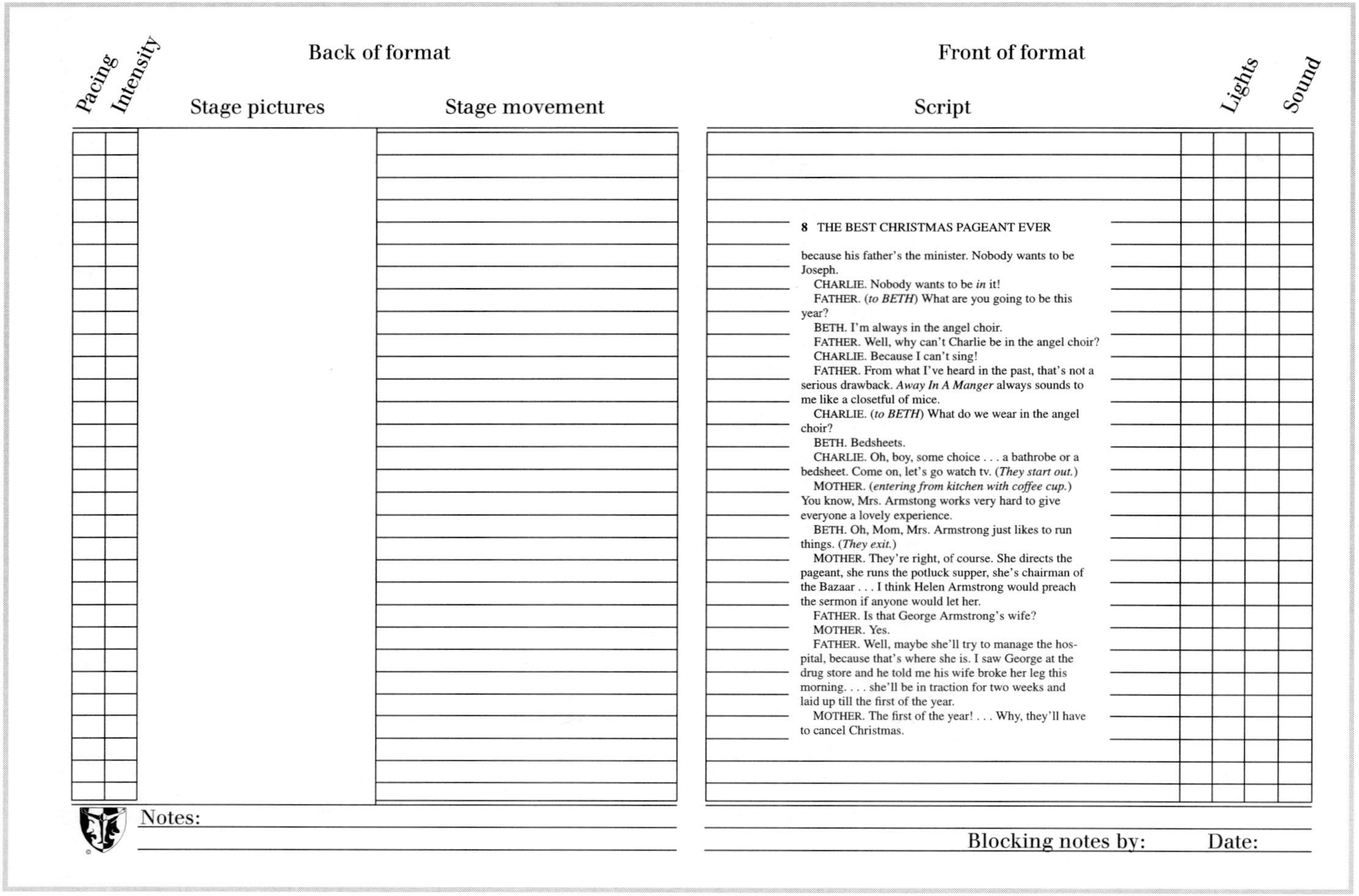

Front of format

Sound | Lights

Script

Stage movement

Back of format

Stage pictures

Pacing | Intensity

Blocking notes by: Date:

Notes:

8 THE BEST CHRISTMAS PAGEANT EVER

because his father's the minister. Nobody wants to be
Joseph.
  CHARLIE. Nobody wants to be *in* it!
  FATHER. (*to BETH*) What are you going to be this
year?
  BETH. I'm always in the angel choir.
  FATHER. Well, why can't Charlie be in the angel choir?
  CHARLIE. Because I can't sing!
  FATHER. From what I've heard in the past, that's not a
serious drawback. *Away In A Manger* always sounds to
me like a closetful of mice.
  CHARLIE. (*to BETH*) What do we wear in the angel
choir?
  BETH. Bedsheets.
  CHARLIE. Oh, boy, some choice . . . a bathrobe or a
bedsheet. Come on, let's go watch tv. (*They start out.*)
  MOTHER. (*entering from kitchen with coffee cup.*)
You know, Mrs. Armstrong works very hard to give
everyone a lovely experience.
  BETH. Oh, Mom, Mrs. Armstrong just likes to run
things. (*They exit.*)
  MOTHER. They're right, of course. She directs the
pageant, she runs the potluck supper, she's chairman of
the Bazaar . . . I think Helen Armstrong would preach
the sermon if anyone would let her.
  FATHER. Is that George Armstrong's wife?
  MOTHER. Yes.
  FATHER. Well, maybe she'll try to manage the hospital, because that's where she is. I saw George at the
drug store and he told me his wife broke her leg this
morning . . . she'll be in traction for two weeks and
laid up till the first of the year.
  MOTHER. The first of the year! . . . Why, they'll have
to cancel Christmas.

Pacing	Intensity	Stage pictures	Stage movement

Notes: _____
_____

Harcourt Brace & Company

Script | Lights | Sound

Blocking notes by:

Date:

Harcourt Brace & Company

FIGURE 4.6

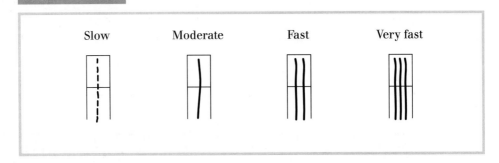

and so on. The director may not say, "This is where the pacing picks up," so you, as stage manager, must be sensitive to changes in pacing and note them when they occur. If you have begun the refining rehearsals and pacing is still irregular from one rehearsal to the next, you should ask the director to identify points of change for you. Do not ask during early rehearsals as this information will probably still be evolving.

Intensity refers to the emotional undercurrents or tensions of the scene. Symbols for this column are repeated and connected lines (see Figure 4-7). Repeated curved lines represent positive intensity (such as joy, relief, love, etc.) and repeated sharply angled lines represent negative intensity (such as anger, frustration, fear, etc.):

You may choose to use this column only to record emotional changes or climaxes when they occur. This information (like pacing) may be illusive and

FIGURE 4.7

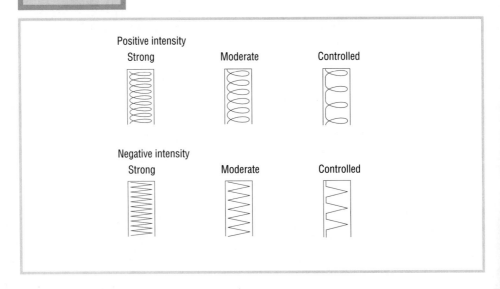

may change from one rehearsal to another. When the interpretation is set, identify the climax or high point of interest in each unit or division of the script and record the points at which the intensity builds, peaks, and ends.

For a short-running show, directors may benefit from this information more than stage managers. However, if you are left to maintain the integrity of the director's concept, you will find these notations invaluable.

Stage pictures are drawings which demonstrate positions on stage or movement from one place to another. Make a copy of the ground plan and reduce it to fit at the top of the stage picture column. Attach it to the original of the notation form so that when you are copying it on the back of your script, the ground plan will also be copied at the same time. Use a circled initial to represent a character, arrows to show direction of movement, and pacing lines to show speed of movement (see Figure 4-8).

FIGURE 4.8

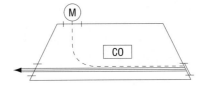

(a) One character movement

Transcription: Mary enters upstage right door, crosses slowly below the couch to the downstage left window, turns and runs to the downstage right door and exits.

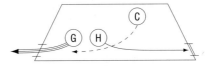

(b) Multiple character movement

Transcription: George exits quickly through downstage right door; Harry crosses to downstage left window; Cindy crosses slowly to downstage right center.

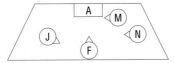

(c) Demonstrating placement and angle of position by adding a 'nose' to each character

Transcription: Father John is downstage center, facing altar, full back to audience; Michael is upstage left center, profile right; Ned is stage left, profile right; Joan is centerstage right, one quarter open.

FIGURE 4.9

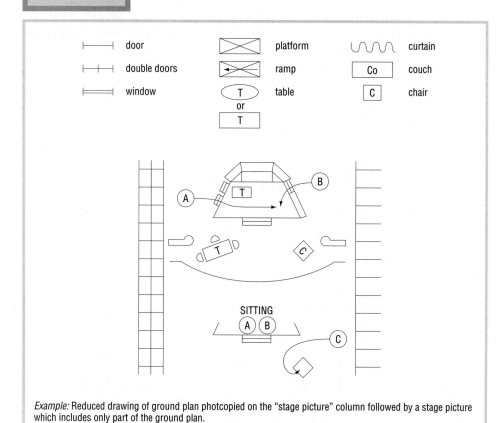

Example: Reduced drawing of ground plan photocopied on the "stage picture" column followed by a stage picture which includes only part of the ground plan.

The stage picture column can also be used to show changes in scenery (walls, platforms, etc.) and properties (moveable objects such as furniture). Draw only that part of the ground plan which will affect the movement or position of a character. For example, your set may be a kitchen with appliances, windows, doors, and so on. However, if all of the activity in a scene takes place around the table, you need not draw in the other props. Props can be designated by initials within a square, a rectangle, or other easily drawn shape which best represents the shape of the object. Some of the symbols in Figure 4-9 are also used for technical drawing.

A stage picture is much faster to draw and to read than written instructions. However, it is not useful for describing movement, gestures, or positions other than the direction a character is facing and the direction and speed of movement. For additional notes, you need words or a symbolic language.

The *stage movement* column has horizontal lines for writing blocking notes or information that cannot be shown in a stage picture. These drawn lines will not necessarily match each typed line of the script on the opposite page since the space between lines of type can vary from one script to another. Additionally, there are often many movements that take place on a single word of dialogue. Therefore, you cannot always write blocking notes opposite the word(s) that cue them. Correlate blocking notes as well as stage pictures with dialogue by numbering them, beginning with the number 1 on each page of script. There might be two blocking notes on a page or there could be twenty or even more (see Figure 4-10).

The *script* column and how to attach the script to the notation form for reproduction is discussed on page 120.

The *lights* and *sound* columns are used for numbering technical cues and correlating them to the script (see Figure 4-10a). There are four columns that may be retitled and used according to the technical demands of the production. Light cues are usually the most abundant in number and may require two or more columns. For example, you might use one column for follow spots, one for the dimmer system, another for sound cues, and the last for flown scenery. If you have more technical cues than these four columns will accomodate, you can add columns or subdivide the original ones. If these solutions do not work for you, abandon these columns and insert the cue sheet (p. 107) between each page of the script or create a new form and make as many columns as you need for your production. These inserts would be used only during technical rehearsals and performances.

Technical cues are continuous. The numbering does not begin anew on each page of script. They (like movement notations) must be identified in the script at the exact place where they occur (see Figure 4-10b). For additional instructions on noting technical cues and calling the show, see Appendix F.

FIGURE 4.10a

Symbols for technical cues: LQ – light cue   > fade out

SQ – sound cue   < fade in

MQ – music cue   >< cross fade

FQ – fly cue

W – warning (call made to alert operator about upcoming cue)

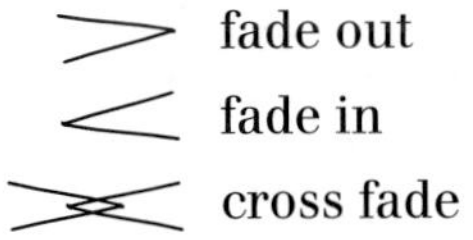

FIGURE 4.10b

EXAMPLE: Demonstrating use of stage pictures, numbering, and correlating movement cues and technical cues

Pacing / Intensity	Stage pictures	Stage movement	Script	Lights	Sound
	1.		FATHER: She's in charge of Christmas? MOTHER: Well, she's in charge of the pageant, and she's in charge of the bazaar.... I feel sorry for Helen, but who's going to do all those things? LQ 12 BLACKOUT → SQ B PHONE RING	#12	
			1.	#8	
			(Lights off stage. Spotlight up DSL on MRS. SLO-CUM, telephoning.) LQ 13 ←	#13	
	2.		MRS. SLOCUM: Yes, I'll take over the bazaar Edna, if you'll do the potluck supper. I don't know what in the world we'll do about the pageant, unless.... How about Grace?		
			2.	#9	
	3.		(Spot off MRS. SLOCUM: spot up DSR on MRS. CLARK, telephoning.) LQ 14 → SQ 9		
			3.	#14	
			MRS. CLARK: I just can't Edna, I've got company all Christmas week.... How about Grace?		
	4.		4.	#10	
			(Spot off MRS. CLARK: Spot up DSL on MRS. CLAUSING, telephoning.) LQ 15 → SQ 10 NONE		
			MRS. CLAUSING.... How about Grace?	#15	
	5.	GL	(Spot off MRS. CLAUSING: Up on MRS. McCAR-THY DSR telephoning.) LQ 16 PHONE SQ 11	#11	
			MRS. McCARTHY: Hello.... Grace...?	#16	
			5.	#17	
		GL	(Spot off MRS. McCARTHY: Stage lights up on living room-dining room set. MOTHER hanging up phone with stunned expression.)	#18	
			6.	#19	
		6. (M) SITS IN [C]	MOTHER: Bob.... LQ 18 ← LQ 19 SL →		

Notes: (S) IN CURLERS (C) IN GREEN FACE MASK

Blocking notes by: _____ Date: _____

Additional *notes* including blocking dates and the initials of the SM can be written at the bottom of the notation graph.

NOTATION SYMBOLS

The idea of learning and reproducing symbols may seem intimidating at first, but they are easy to draw and to remember. Most of the symbols look like the movement, position, or object they represent. A quick example should ease your mind about the ease of learning and using this system.

First, look at the symbols for each of the following words:

EN	enter	t	turn
EX	exit	⌒	pause
→	to	♭	below

Here are blocking notes using words:

Mary enters upstage right door, crosses slowly below the table to downstage left window, pauses 3 seconds, turns and runs to downstage right door, exits.

Here are the same blocking notes using symbols:

Ⓜ EN UR ⊢⊣, --→ ♭ ⟦T⟧ ⟿ DL ⊢⊣, 3 ⌒, t ⇛ ⟿ DR ⊢⊣, EX

Can you transcribe the following notation? The answer is at the bottom of the page*.

Ⓜ EN UC ⊢⊣, ⇒ ♭ ⟦CO⟧ ⟿ ⊠ A, ⌒, t --→ ⟿ DR ⊢⊣, EX

You have now been introduced to the concept, the format, and thirty symbols in the Schneider Notation System. The remainder are just as easy to learn.

Obviously, every word does not have a symbol. When a word is used which has no symbol, or if you cannot recall the symbol for a word, write the word or abbreviate it very clearly. A long line of notations with words interspersed is easier to transcribe than one which has only symbols (see the following line of notation).

Ⓜ SKIPS ⟿ ⟦C⟧, LAUGHS, 2 ⌒ & FAINTS ♭ ⟦C⟧

Use block lettering to write all words and abbreviations (see Appendix B). Personal writing style can decrease legibility.

If a word without a representative symbol is used repeatedly in rehearsals, create a symbol for it. Add this new symbol to your symbol key (see p. 140) so others will be able to transcribe your notes. The simplest approach to creating a new symbol is to use abbreviations (see Figure 4-11). If it is a property, put the initials inside a shape which best represents it, but do not use a circle as that may be confused with a character's name.

---

*Answer: Mary enters upstage center window, quickly crosses below couch to platform A, pauses, turns and slowly crosses to downstage right door, exits.

FIGURE 4.11

EXAMPLE: MB music box
           S   swing (noun)
           SWG swing (verb)

The symbols of the Schneider Notation System are separated into five divisions:

1. movement and direction
2. positions and gestures
3. anatomy
4. unarmed combat*
5. dance**

These divisions include worksheets for practice in drawing the symbols followed by transcription exercises. To make the new symbols easier to remember, each division has between four and ten base symbols which may be added to or changed slightly to represent words with related meanings (see Figure 4-12).

The following pages introduce the remaining symbols and provide opportunities to practice drawing and transcribing them. The symbols are drawn within squares in order to demonstrate spatial proportions and to encourage consistency in use of space. Use a pencil to fill out the worksheets and transcriptions. Look at each symbol to visually note its proportions within the square. A dot (•) is placed on each sample drawing to identify the best place to begin the symbol; however, do not include the dot in your practice drawings or transcriptions.

It is important to draw each symbol in order to remember it. Most symbols are designed to be drawn from the left to the right and with as few strokes of the pencil as possible. Using the following recommendations will facilitate your task.

---

*Symbols and formats for noting unarmed stage combat are discussed in Chapter 5. Words and symbols for unarmed combat can also be used in noncombat scenes: for example, trip (on a rug), fall (onto a couch), kick (an object), stomp (to make a point).

**Dance notation will be discussed in Chapter 6.

FIGURE 4.12

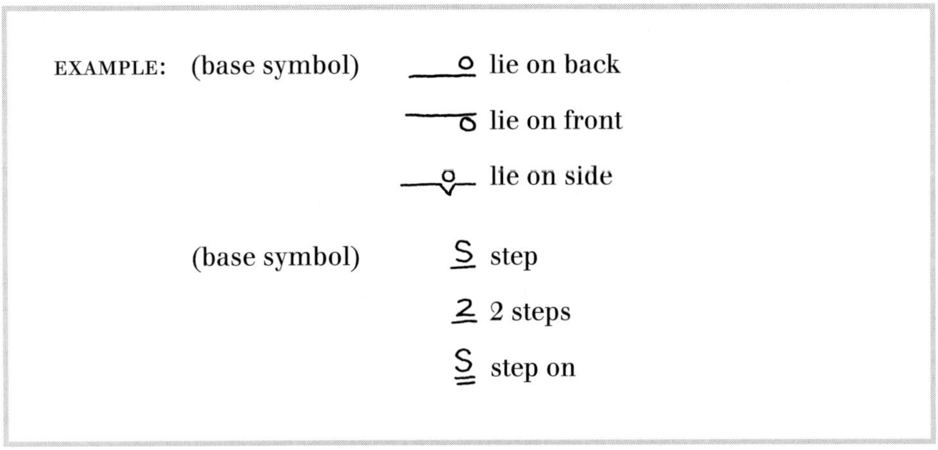

EXAMPLE: (base symbol)   o̲ lie on back

                                    ō̄ lie on front

                                    o̲ lie on side

            (base symbol)   S̲ step

                                    2̲ 2 steps

                                    S̲̲ step on

1. *Use the worksheets* to learn the symbols prior to blocking rehearsals.

2. Begin using symbols at the first blocking rehearsal. *Do not plan to incorporate the symbols into your notations later.* "Later" never comes. One purpose of the symbols is to add speed, not extra work, to the process of noting blocking.

3. *Do not stop rehearsal to search for a symbol you cannot remember.* Use words which can be replaced by the forgotten symbols after rehearsal.

4. *Do stop rehearsal if the blocking is unclear* or if it varies from what you have previously written. Your notes must reflect any changes or modifications.

5. You need a desk or hard writing surface and adequate light so that your writing is not restricted by space limitations or discomfort. *Easy legibility is second only to accuracy.*

6. *Be sure your ASM can use your system,* read your notes, and call the show.

7. *Always use a medium lead (HB) or (H) pencil for notating blocking.* Lines made by a pencil with a soft lead will smear when erased; pencils with harder leads (2H or 3H) produce light lines which are difficult to read in dim lighting. A mechanical pencil is desirable as it never needs sharpening and maintains a consistent line width. Keep additional erasers handy. The eraser on your pencil will wear out before the pencil does.

Many symbols can be modified by adding or changing a number, and additional symbols can be created by following a previously established pattern.

EXAMPLE: $\underline{2}$ two steps

                3⌢   three second pause

                ←--   back slowly

                ⇐   back quickly

                ⇚   run backwards

NOTE: The symbols for "start," "speed up," "slow down," and "stop" can also be used in the dialogue to guide changes in rate of verbal delivery.

A line beneath a symbol means "on"; a line above a symbol means "off."

⌒‾ hop on   ‾⌄‾ hop off   ⊢ turn on

Use only those symbols necessary for clarity.

Abe crosses slowly to downstage left and exits through door.

overkill: Ⓐ ✕ --→ ⟶ DL ✦ EX ⊖⟳ ⊢⊣

simpler to draw and easier to read: Ⓐ --→ ⟶ DL ⊢⊣ , EX

                                or

                Ⓐ --→ EX DL ⊢⊣

Most of the position and gesture symbols are not easy to use in stage pictures. However, the symbols may be incorporated or used beside the stage picture.

Amy enters upstage right door, sneaking between the tables, pauses above chair 2, and then rushes to Mary who is profile left. Amy touches Mary's back and Mary jumps, dropping the vase.

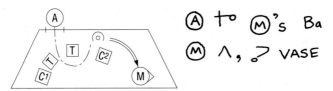

Ⓐ t⁰ Ⓜ's Ba

Ⓜ ∧ , ⟋ VASE

Some symbols can cause confusion about who is doing what to whom.

Sally sits beside John and he puts his arm around her.

Not clear: Ⓢ ⸕)(Ⓙ ⟲

Clear: Ⓢ ⸕)(Ⓙ , Ⓙ ⟲ Ⓢ

NOTE: To make noun symbols plural, add a number or an s.

Movement and Direction Symbols and Worksheet

Base symbols: ◸ start   →| walk |S| step   ⋀ hop

⌐→| to   ⌐T turn

◸ start						⌐→| to					
◸ speed up						↽ from					
◺ slow down						⌐↘ back & forth					
◿ stop						↱ up & down					
→ walk						⊥ above, behind					
⇒ walk fast						T below, in front					
⇛ run						(O) over					
--→ walk slowly						(O) under					
⋯ creep, sneak						(O) around					
← back up						⊖ through					
◠ circle						⊖ in					
⑤ spin						⊖ out					
◇ pace						⌐T turn					
ℒ follow						◹ 1/4 turn					
S step						◹ 1/2 turn					
⋀ hop						◖ 3/4 turn					
⌢ leap						◗ full turn					
⋀ jump											
△ jump on											
⩓ jump off											

MOVEMENT AND DIRECTION SYMBOLS	TRANSCRIPTION EXERCISE A

Transcribe the following symbols into stage directions. It is not wrong unless it cannot be interpreted accurately. Put symbols in an order that will make interpretation easy. If actions occur sequentially, use a comma or an ampersand to separate them. If they occur simultaneously, use "wh" for "while" or precede each action with "-" and stack them (see answer 8). (Answers to this and the other exercises are at the end of the chapter.)

1. ⑤ EX ↳ DL ∿∿

2. ⑧ ↺ ↟ COFFEE [T] or ⑧ ↺ ↟ [CT]

3. ⑩ ↺ ③̂ , ⑩ EX ⟹ UR ⊢—⊣

4. Ⓜ ↺ , ⟹ UC LAUGHING

5. ⑩ ⟹ ⤳ [CO] , ⌒ △ , LK ⤸ , LK ↩ C CUSHION

Transcribe the following stage directions into symbols:

6. Mary kicks platform, then hops up and down while crying.

7. John jumps off table and kneels in full front position.

8. Ann spins while John paces and Bill slowly exits at the upstage right door.

9. Joe enters stage right, pauses, and then sneaks through stage left door.

10. Bill crosses four steps to Joe; Joe turns, leaps over small table, and exits above stage right curtain. Bill follows.

Can stage pictures replace any of the above? If so, draw them.

Position and Gesture Symbols and Worksheet

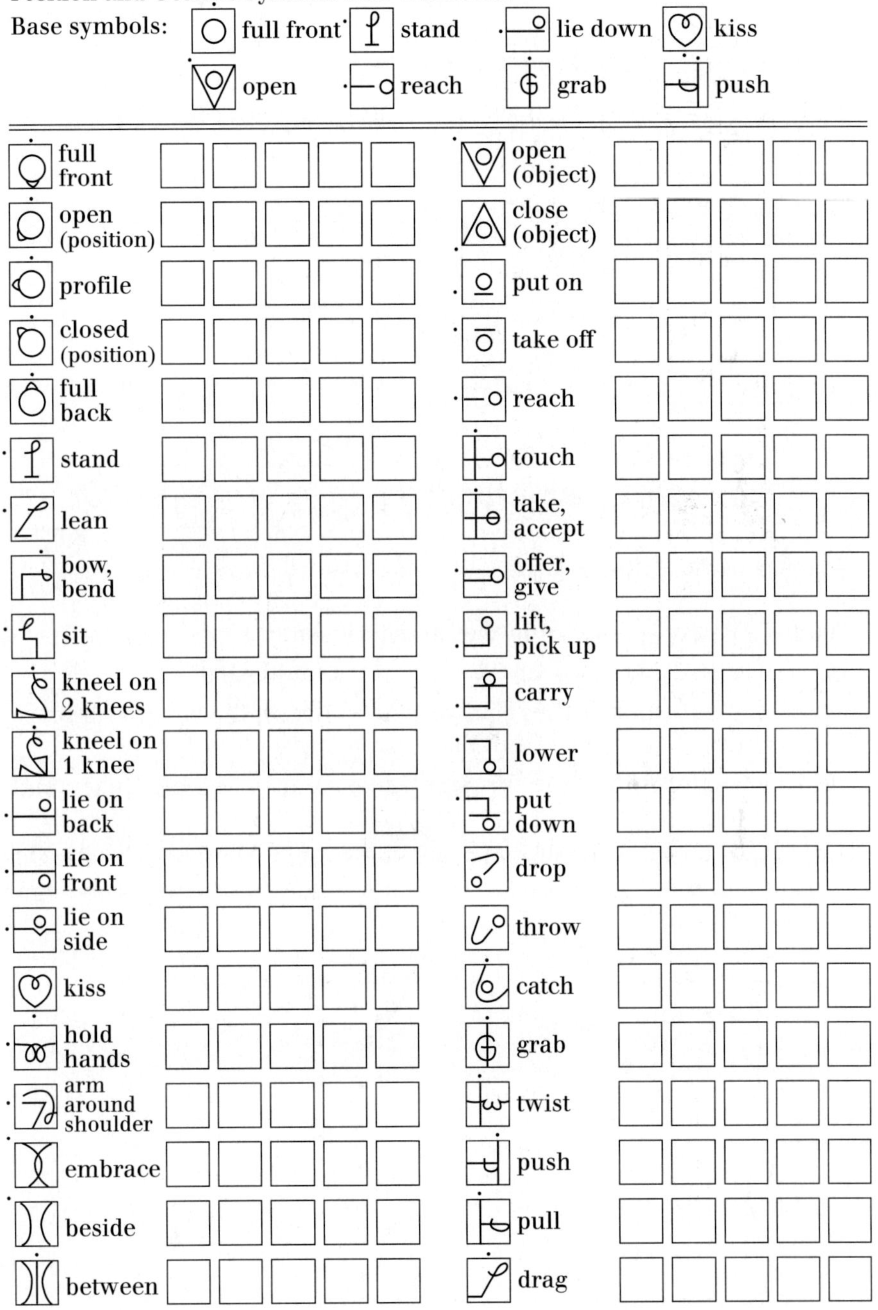
Base symbols:
full front
stand
lie down
kiss
open
reach
grab
push
full front
open (position)
profile
closed (position)
full back
stand
lean
bow, bend
sit
kneel on 2 knees
kneel on 1 knee
lie on back
lie on front
lie on side
kiss
hold hands
arm around shoulder
embrace
beside
between
open (object)
close (object)
put on
take off
reach
touch
take, accept
offer, give
lift, pick up
carry
lower
put down
drop
throw
catch
grab
twist
push
pull
drag

POSITION AND GESTURE SYMBOLS	TRANSCRIPTION EXERCISE B

Transcribe the following symbols into stage directions. When a character begins an action, assume the continuing notes refer to additional actions by the same character unless you identify another character as initiating a movement (see answer 8 of the answers to exercise B found at the end of the chapter).

1. (J) ⟹)|([T] + [ca] J̊ DISHES

2. (M) ⌐)((G) ON [co]

3. (A) J̊ (C) ⟶ [SW] , ⌿

4. (J)✗)|([T] + [C] , ⟋ (◁))(HAT RACK

5. (J) ⌐ᵇ ⟶ (M) + ♡ARMS, (M) ← s, t ◁, ō RING +?

Transcribe the following stage directions into symbols:

6. John runs to Mary, embraces and kisses her.
7. Mary sits beside Ann and helps her put on her hat.
8. The King leans on the table, facing full front; the Knight removes his helmet and kneels, full back to audience.
9. The Knight stands and the King backs up between the Queen and Jester.
10. The Jester lies down on his side below the throne and the Knight puts on his helmet, closes the visor, and the Queen throws her scarf to him.

Can stage pictures replace any of the above? If so, draw them.

Anatomy Symbols and Worksheet

Base symbols: head, face   front torso   arm   leg

Symbol							Symbol					
head, face							upper back					
nose							kidney					
eyes							buttocks					
mouth							arm					
back of head							shoulder					
side of head							elbow					
hair							forearm					
neck, throat							wrist					
front torso							hand					
back torso							leg					
chest							thigh					
ribs							knee					
stomach, waist							shin					
belly							ankle					
groin							foot					

The anatomy symbols are especially easy to remember because, when put together, they look like a stick figure. After seeing and drawing our character below, you will not only find it easy to remember, you will find it difficult to forget.

ANATOMY SYMBOLS	TRANSCRIPTION EXERCISE C

Transcribe the following symbols into stage directions. Some of the anatomy symbols are used primarily in stage combat (such as those for "kidney," "groin," and "ribs").

1. Ⓜ COVERS ♀ W 2 ♈

2. Ⓢ ⌐⁶ HOLDING ⚔

3. Ⓙ ≤ Ⓑ Ⓨ

4. Ⓜ ◡° BRUSH + HITS Ⓓ ♀

5. Ⓐ ¢ Ⓙ ↘ wh Ⓙ ĵ GUN + POINTS AT Ⓐ

Transcribe the following stage directions into symbols:

6. John touches Jane's arm.

7. Bill tickles Sally's foot. She jumps up and reaches for his hand. He grabs her wrist.

8. John touches his chest, drops to his knees, and falls on the stage, face down.

9. John twists his ankle, kneels on one knee, removes his shoe, and rubs his foot.

10. Moe picks up a pie from the table and throws it at Curley's face. Curley turns full front and wipes his face, picks up glass, and crosses to Moe. He throws the drink on Moe's front.

SYMBOL KEY

The *symbol key* includes all of the symbols of the Schneider Notation System. On the bottom line are boxes with blank lines beside them. If you need additional symbols for for a production, draw and label them in these spaces. For example, if a music box is an important prop and often is referred to in blocking, you would use a shape which represents the object and put its initials inside the shape.

music box   [MB]

Likewise, if there is a repeated movement that does not have a symbol and is too long to write each time it occurs, create a representative symbol. For example, if your production requires movements unique to a culture or time such as "genuflect" (a Catholic ritual gesture used in *Murder in the Cathedral*) or "kow-tow" (a posture of submission used in *The Mikado* or *The King and I*), use an abbreviation or draw a symbol which suggests the movement.

genuflect   GEN. or ♀

kow-tow   K-T or Z

Insert a copy of the symbol key (found on the next page) in your production book. It will be an easy reference for blocking rehearsals and will aid in future transcriptions of the book.

SYMBOL KEY
Schneider Notation System

Symbol	Meaning	Symbol	Meaning	Symbol	Meaning	Symbol	Meaning	Symbol	Meaning
	start		back & forth		bow, bend		carry		ribs
	speed up		up & down		sit		lower		stomach, waist
	slow down		above, behind		kneel on 2 knees		put down		belly
	stop		below, in front		kneel on 1 knee		drop		groin
	walk		over		lie on back		throw		upper back
	walk fast		under		lie on front		catch		kidney
	run		around		lie on side		grab		buttocks
	walk slowly		through		kiss		twist		arm
	creep, sneak		in		hold hands		push		shoulder
	back up		out		arm around shoulder		pull		elbow
	circle		turn		embrace		drag		forearm
	spin		1/4 turn		beside		head, face		wrist
	pace		1/2 turn		between		nose		hand
	follow		3/4 turn		open (object)		eyes		leg
	step		full turn		close (object)		mouth		thigh
	hop		full front		put on		back of head		knee
	leap		open (position)		take off		side of head		shin
	jump		profile		reach		hair		ankle
	jump on		closed (position)		touch		neck, throat		foot
	jump off		full back		take, accept		front torso		
	to		stand		offer, give		back torso		
	from		lean		lift, pick up		chest		

140

EXERCISE ANSWERS

A.

1. Sally exits below the downstage left curtain.

2. Bill paces above the coffee table.

3. Jane is in a full back position. John circles her, then exits quickly through the upstage right door.

4. Mary makes a three-quarter turn, then runs upstage center, laughing.

5. John runs to couch, pauses with full back to audience, looks back and forth, then looks under the center cushion.

6.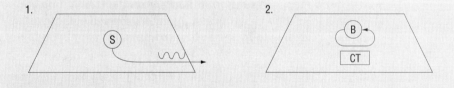

7.

8.

9.

10.

Transcriptions 1, 2, 3, and 9 can be drawn as stage pictures.

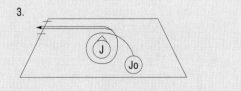

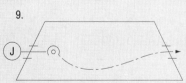

EXERCISE ANSWERS

B.

1. Jane runs between table and cabinet, carrying dishes.

2. Mother sits beside Grandmother on the couch.

3. Abe carries the child to the swing, and puts her down.

4. John crosses between the table and chair and stops beside the hat rack in a left profile position.

5. John bows to Mary and opens his arms. She takes one step back, turns right profile, removes her ring and drops it.

6. Ⓙ X ⟹ ⟶ Ⓜ, ⅄ ← ♡

7. Ⓜ ⤵)(Ⓐ, HELPS Ⓐ ⊇ HAT

8. Ⓚ ∠ ON ⌑T⌐, Ⓚɴ ō HELMET, N° ⚬

9. Ⓚɴ ι, Ⓚ ←)|(Ⓠ ← Ⓙ

10. Ⓙ —℘— ↾ THRONE + Ⓚɴ ⊇ HELMET, ⋏VISOR, Ⓠ ∪ SCARF ⟶ Ⓚɴ

NOTE: Transcriptions 2 and 4 can be represented by stage pictures.

2.

4.
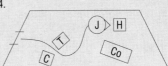

EXERCISE ANSWERS

C.

1. Mary covers her face with both hands.
2. Sally bends over, holding her stomach.
3. Jim steps on Bob's neck.
4. Molly throws a brush and hits Dan on the back of his head.
5. Amy grabs Jim's leg while Jim raises the gun and points it at Amy.
6. (handwritten stage notation)
7. (handwritten stage notation) ⓑ TICKLES ⓢ, ⓢ ∧—○ FOR ⓑ, ⓑ ⓢ
8. (handwritten stage notation) ⓙ to 𝕏, —►'s, FALLS —○
9. (handwritten stage notation) ⓙ TWISTS, Ō SHOE + RUBS
10. (handwritten stage notation) Ⓜ PIE — 🔲, PIE —► ©, © + WIPES, © GLASS, X —► Ⓜ, DRINK ON Ⓜ 𝕏

STAGE MANAGING
STAGE COMBAT

Stage combat is the most dangerous activity in which actors participate. It is a physical discipline requiring artistically designed choreography. It gives the illusion of spontaneous, violent, and aggressive competition, but must be the result of well-rehearsed, controlled, and cooperative movement. It may range from a lover's slap to a sword fight to a barroom brawl with gunfire. Everyone has heard the story of actor Brandon Lee's accidental death while filming *The Crow.* There are so many accidents and injuries associated with work in the theatre. The most serious are usually related to stage combat. An informed and conscientious stage manager, who assists with communicating and enforcing safety regulations and supervises combat warm-ups and rehearsals, can improve performances and prevent injuries.

> *After the Fight Master has gone his merry way, the Stage Manager takes on the role of referee for stage fights in rehearsal and performance. In disputes over who is "right" or "wrong," the SM is the neutral party that reestablishes balance and harmony. Whatever the differences of opinion among combatants, many an injury has been avoided because the SM has faithfully seen to it that combat safety remains everyone's priority.*
>
> —J. D. MARTINEZ, FIGHT MASTER, DIRECTOR AND AUTHOR,
> WASHINGTON AND LEE UNIVERSITY

Keep in mind that a little knowledge can be dangerous. This chapter does not replace formal hands-on training. There are numerous sources for increasing your knowledge and improving your skills in combat and the use of firearms on stage. The first choice is workshops with qualified trainers. Some very good supplements or alternatives include videos which can also be used in

Actors Tim Klotz (left) and J. D. Martinez rehearse a sword duel at Shakespeare's Globe Theatre on the South Bank of the Thames in London. (Photo by Lewis Shaw)

safety training sessions for your cast and crews, and well-illustrated books. A recommended sample of each includes the following:

> *Firearm Safety Onstage* with Robert B. Chambers. Theatre Arts Video Library, 174 Andrew Avenue, Leucadia, CA, 92024. 1992.

> *Unarmed Stage Combat I: Learning the Basics with David Leong and J. Allen Suddeth.* Combat Masters, International, Inc., P.O. Box 1321, Roslyn Heights, NY, 11577.

> *Combat Mime, A Non-Violent Approach to Stage Violence,* by J. D. Martinez; illustrated by Caren Caraway. Chicago: Nelson-Hall, 1988.

THE STAGE COMBAT STAFF

The *fight director* is responsible for choreographing and rehearsing fight scenes. He or she may be with the company only for as long as it takes to block the fights and bring them up to performance quality. The fight captain or the stage manager is then left with the job of supervising the remaining rehearsals and performances and maintaining the integrity of the original choreography.

A *fight captain* may be appointed to assist with warm-ups and rehearsals and maintenance and security of weapons. If qualified, the ASM may take this role; otherwise, one of the combatants may be assigned these duties, or they may fall to the stage manager. Do not attempt this role until you have the information or training necessary to carry it out safely. However, having a fight captain does not eliminate the need for the stage manager at combat rehearsals. You must be familiar with the choreography in order to troubleshoot during performances and give notes after performances.

A **pyrotechnic** may be hired for supervising the use of firearms or explosives, but if the budget does not allow for an additional staff person, there are alternatives. The fight director or fight captain may be experienced with firearms and can fulfill the role; the police department may be willing to assist with arms and instruction; or a recognized expert in the community may volunteer his/her services. Some states require the presence of a licensed pyrotechnician if any cartridges other than blanks are used or if black powder (above an established measure) is used. The regulations differ from state to state, from city to county and from indoor to outdoor use. The local fire marshal can answer questions concerning the law, licensing, and safety.

The stage manager's role in stage combat may include some or all of the following:

- Assisting with auditions for fight scenes
- Collaborating with all designers about combat needs in early production meetings
- Running safe and accurate rehearsals and performances
- Maintaining proper care, handling, and security of weapons
- Notating fight sequences
- Warming up fighters before performances

AUDITIONS

Stage combat is rarely included in auditions, even for those roles which require advanced fighting skills. An actor's resumé information on training in armed and unarmed combat is usually sufficient. If an actor is a member of The Society of American Fight Directors (SAFD), that should be in the resumé and will be recognized by most producers and directors as verification of a performer's knowledge of mimed combat.

If, however, it is necessary to ascertain the level of an actor/combatant's skill, the procedure most commonly used is the same as that of a dance choreographer. The fight director teaches the combatants a short combination of moves, establishes some kind of rhythm and tempo, and observes the resulting performance.

The stage manager should know in advance if auditions will include combat and bring appropriate props and equipment for the actors. These may include mats, masks, padding, and weapons. Be sure appropriate footwear is worn and floors are clean and nonslippery. Have combatants warm up before auditioning and be alert to potential danger due to excess enthusiasm. An actor may take abnormal risks in an audition in an effort to prove capability and to compete for a role.

PRODUCTION MEETINGS

The *fight director* should attend early production meetings and should collaborate with the director and all designers about costume, prop, and scenery needs for safe rehearsal and performance of fight sequences. The SM notes all decisions and follows up (with the assistance of the fight director) by preparing lists of rehearsal needs and procurement deadlines for the appropriate staff members. The fight director should also state the number of hours required to master the choreography so that adequate rehearsal time is scheduled on the master calendar.

The *producer* should discuss legal liability for injuries resulting from stage combat or use of firearms or explosives with the cast and crews.

The *director* may want characterization built into fight sequences and special effects or subtle actions which help communicate mood and script interpretation. The SM should note all verbal concepts which might assist the fight director and help maintain the integrity of the choreography in later rehearsals.

The *scenery design* (especially varied levels and set props) will affect the use of space in choreography. All scenery which will be involved in fight sequences should be evaluated for safety prior to and, again, after construction. Staircases, in particular, require sufficient **tread** depth and width and support walls or railings to assure safe combat use. Floor and platform surfaces should also be discussed to avoid slippery or splintery finishes, and noise of combat should be taken into consideration. Padded floors are often the best solution and can cut down on the combatants' body padding which must be masked by costumes. Openings through which combatants must exit (while fighting) should be sufficiently large and clear of stored scenery. Platforms and set props used in combat should be scheduled for completion during early rehearsals.

Weapons as well as *hand and set props* that may be used as weapons (including special effects such as **breakaway** bottles or chairs) should also be discussed and made available for rehearsals. The style, construction material, and number of weapons should be determined. If weapons are used in hand-to-hand battle, they are at risk of being broken. Request several replacement weapons in anticipation of loss due to breakage or theft. Procure a lockable storage place for these props to prevent abuse, theft, or injury.

If *firearms* are to be used (even one single shot fired), insist on rigid guidelines for selecting, handling, firing, cleaning, and storing these weapons. This includes the recruitment of a pyrotechnician or other expert to teach and supervise all of the above. The use of firearms may also affect costumes and scenery, requiring fire safety devices, fire-proofing techniques, and extinguishers (see Chapter 7).

The *costume designs* should be evaluated for freedom of movement and their ability to accommodate any padding needed for protection of combatants. Some period styles restrict movement and would therefore influence choreography. Likewise, padding might spoil the line of a period costume and would require special design consideration. If costume pieces are to be ripped, bloodied, or otherwise used as a part of combat, the details should be discussed and rehearsal costumes made available to set timing so these special effects will smoothly interlace with the action. Any other costume pieces or protective padding which may affect the safety of a fight sequence should also be added to the list of rehearsal costumes, including such things as capes, long garments, scabbards or holsters, footwear, gloves, armor, helmets, hats, masks, and so on.

Sound effects or *music* may cue, accompany, or establish the rhythm and tempo of fight choreography. These must be planned before rehearsals and used as soon as the fight is up to tempo.

The *lighting design* should be discussed to determine any special effects which might affect a combatant's vision, such as a strobe light, bright **backlighting,** deeply shadowed areas, or a very low level of intensity. Any lighting effects which might create a hazard must be made available during rehearsals.

REHEARSALS AND PERFORMANCES

Stage combat and the use of firearms are the most dangerous activities which take place on stage. There is no way to make combat or the use of firearms absolutely safe, but there are many things which can be done to lessen the danger. The following list of safety guidelines will assist you in minimizing hazards and risks.

SAFETY GUIDELINES FOR COMBAT

1. If stage combat is new to your company, review the potential dangers with the director and designers and review their roles in protecting the actors.
2. If stage combat is new to the actors, either you or the fight director should discuss safety guidelines.

3. In planning the rehearsal schedule, allow a block of time each day for combat rehearsal. Simply rehearsing fight sequences as you get to them in the script is not sufficient. The amount of time needed for each rehearsal depends on the number and duration of the fight sequences and should be determined by the fight director.

> *I have great respect for the Stage Manager who can successfully juggle the demands of many masters. I remember one SM, however, who forced a stop to an under-rehearsed stage fight, in spite of my professional opinion, because of an arbitrary rehearsal schedule that had been devised weeks before rehearsals began. I therefore felt obligated to write a letter to the theatre's insurance company absolving myself from all responsibility for any injuries that might result from lack of adequate preparation. Needless to say, the theatre's management (and their Board of Directors) were not happy. In that case, the SM failed to serve any master.*
>
> —J. D. MARTINEZ, FIGHT MASTER, DIRECTOR, AUTHOR

4. Schedule all platforms and other levels (staircases, windows, etc.) that will be used in fight sequences for early completion in order to have as much rehearsal time with them as possible. This includes padding.

5. Arrange for necessary floor mats and protective clothing (pads, masks, etc.) to be available at each rehearsal.

6. See that all set and hand props (or exact replicas) that are to be used in the fight sequences are available for use early in rehearsals.

7. Request and secure all rehearsal weapons. They should be the same weapons (or replicas of them) that will be used in performance. Assign the care and handling to an ASM or to the actor that uses them.

   ■ Have an expert demonstrate the proper way to check a weapon for safe use.

   ■ Be sure all blades are blunted and tipped. Examine them regularly for damage.

   ■ Wrap handles to avoid slipping due to a poor grip or perspiration.

   ■ Check all joined parts for tightness and all movable parts for proper action.

   ■ Any prop that is used as a weapon (such as scissors or a hairbrush) *is* a weapon and must be given the same careful treatment.

8. See that all rehearsal costumes which affect movement, vision, or timing in fight scenes (such as long garments, capes, scabbards, helmets, etc.) are available early in rehearsals. These should be the costumes which will be used in performance or an exact replica. A slight change in weight or flow can affect timing and become a hazard.

9. Be sure the rehearsal space is properly heated or cooled and the floor is swept and checked for staples, nails, splintering, and so on before each rehearsal.

10. Assign the fight captain or a combatant to lead warm-ups before each rehearsal and performance. The fight director should plan warm-ups appropriate to the type of combat used. A common approach is to begin with stretching exercises followed by a walk-through of each fight sequence, maintaining the rhythm but slowing the tempo. A combatant should never be allowed to fight without first warming up. You or an ASM also should be present for warm-ups because the fight captain is probably one of the combatants.

11. If music or sound effects are to be used (as background or as the actual rhythm and tempo of the fight), have the tape available at all rehearsals. If the combatants have lines to deliver above the sound effects or music, set sound levels to accommodate their dialogue.

12. Combat rehearsals will begin at a slow pace until the combatants have learned the sequence, the rhythm, and (gradually) the tempo. Never let the combatants speed up a fight until it is perfected. In outdoor theatre, the weather may create problems for a performance without being bad enough to stop the show. In such a situation, the audience will understand (if they notice) a slowing of the fight tempo for the sake of safety.

13. Whenever a combatant shows loss of temper, patience, or concentration, the fight should be stopped. An injury is pending. If *anything* seems wrong (a change in timing or rhythm, a possible injury, or a damaged weapon or prop), stop the fight.

14. Combat rehearsals should include bystanders (at least for a time long enough to anticipate problems and to define combat space). Bystanders must be blocked as they will probably have to **give stage** (get out of the way) for moving combatants, providing a safe distance for the use of weapons and for choreography.

15. Have preplanned signals (a verbal cue which combatants can give to one another as a warning or distress signal or a sound or light cue which can be given by the stage manager) for stopping a fight during performance. An injured actor may want to continue the fight in the traditional "the-show-must-go-on" attitude. This must never be allowed. Continuing to move with an injury may worsen the injury. Better an abbreviated performance than an abbreviated performer. Emphasize the combatants' responsibilities to themselves and to each other.

16. If a fight which is to end with injury or death must be stopped before its conclusion, have an alternative ending planned so that the continuity of the script is not broken. Also, a gun might misfire or a knife might be dropped, requiring an alternative weapon to finish the scene. Anticipate problems and rehearse alternatives so that they can be safely carried out.

17. Always keep a first-aid kit available and give immediate care to injuries (see Chapter 7). Most injuries cannot wait until after a rehearsal or performance.

> *I was stage managing for a classical repertory company and we were rehearsing a fight with broadswords prior to a performance. One of the lead character/fighters got sliced on his nose. We had to stop rehearsals and take him to the best plastic surgeon which was forty miles away. We had people calling ahead, alerting the hospital, so we could get him stitched and back in time for the show. I also called the [assistant] stage manager so she could begin prepping the understudy. We got back fifteen minutes before curtain and he made his entrance (in costume, make-up, and wig) as the first character on stage.*

> —EVELYN MATTEN, AEA STAGE MANAGER, AMERICAN PLAYERS THEATRE

18. Secure all weapons in a locked space after rehearsals or performances. If you are doing outdoor theatre, be sure the weapons are locked in a climate-controlled place.
19. Keep a repair sheet (p. 110) backstage and in the dressing rooms. Ask combatants to list and circle any damaged weapon, prop, or costume piece used in a fight. Make sure the repair is completed before the next rehearsal or performance.

SAFETY GUIDELINES FOR FIREARMS

Before making any decisions about firearms in your production, check all local and regional firearms laws. If you plan to tour the show, check state and federal regulations regarding transportation of guns across state lines. Your local police station can provide answers or directions for finding answers.

Firearms vary in construction, style, and ammunition as well as in the procedures for loading, firing, unloading, and cleaning. Not only must they be realistic in look and sound for the period of history they represent, but the powder load (which controls the volume of sound) must be gauged to suit the size and **acoustics** of the theatre. Naturally, live ammunition is replaced with blanks, but even blanks can vary and are dangerous. The powder which makes the explosive sound can burn; and the paper wadding which replaces the bullet is still a projectile which can kill if improperly used.

There are five major steps which must be taken to minimize the danger of firearms:

1. Select appropriate and safe firearms.

   ■ Prop and gun rental houses can be helpful in selecting the proper gun for your production. They may carry replicas of guns which are "dummys" (do not fire at all) or which have been "baffled" (fire blanks which are released through an opening other than the end of the barrel). Specially built firearms can be expensive, but your budget should be prioritized to protect the health and safety of your cast and crew.

- Black powder guns such as muskets are, in some ways, safer because the amount of powder used can be controlled. In other ways, they are more dangerous because they are unpredictable. It is still safest to use a dummy onstage and a blank-firing starter pistol offstage. In order to maintain the illusion of reality, flash paper can be used as wadding and (when fired) will produce a blaze and smoke like a real period weapon.

- In purchasing blanks, be sure to get the style and powder load appropriate for your weapon and your performance space. Construction tool blanks are more powerful than the ordinary blank and can damage your weapon as well as the shooter. Military blanks should never be used indoors because of the volume of sound they produce. Wadless blanks are available now which do not cause damage.

- Do not try to baffle or alter a weapon.

- Do not use personal firearms unless they have been tested and proven safe.

- Never use a live weapon onstage when a nonfiring replica will do.

2. Arrange a training session for the cast and stage crews.

- Have a firearms expert demonstrate the use of each weapon, including loading, firing, unloading, cleaning, and safe storage and transport.

- Test each weapon for the discharge pattern and penetration power. (Fire the gun beside a sheet of white paper and check the spread of powder released; fire the gun so the wadding released from the blank is aimed at the paper. Note the force of the wadding by the damage to the paper). Use eye and ear protection (goggles and earplugs or earmuffs developed for this purpose) while testing.

- Have the shooter and target actors go through the steps of loading, unloading, and cleaning the gun. It is common practice for the target actor to load the gun and have possession of it (or give it to the stage manager or ASM) until time for its use.

An ASM was responsible for cleaning and loading blanks in a pistol. He delegated someone else to unload it one night. A blank was left in the firing chamber by mistake. The next day, the ASM pulled it out to clean it and blew part of his finger off.

—CRAIG WEINDLING, AEA STAGE MANAGER

■ Review all safety guidelines and regulations concerning the use of firearms and then post them.

3. Be sure the director is aware of safety guidelines associated with positioning and blocking shooters, targets, and bystanders while firearms are in use onstage.

■ Never point a gun at *anyone.* Your hand will naturally aim where you are looking, so sight on something else. The rule is to point the gun **upstage** of the target and do not ever point at the audience. Even blanks can kill if there is a projectile released from an open barrel, so firing into the **wings** can be dangerous if an actor or crew member is standing there. Plan the line of fire; mark it on the floor; and make every actor and member of the running crew aware of it. *Also,* test this firing position to see where the spent and ejected shell or wadding goes. It may land in the auditorium, on flammable fabric, and so on.

■ A gun should never be fired next to a person's head. The sound can be temporarily deafening, especially in a closed space. One recommendation for avoiding damage is to keep your mouth open, lessening the impact of the sound; another is to wear soft ear plugs (hearing suppressors). Do not use hard ear plugs. Also, baffled guns may discharge blanks to the side making this a dangerous position for a bystander or crew member.

■ Do not block an actor to drop or throw a working firearm. It can damage the firing mechanism and cause it to misfire or to fire accidentally.

■ If a gun must be held to someone's head, use a dummy (in place of the gun or the actor). Seriously, no one wants a bullet-firing or a blank-firing gun held to their head. Even if the powder and wadding went in a safe direction, the sound would not.

4. Develop and post a list of guidelines, warnings, and regulations concerning firearm safety to be read and followed by cast and crew. *All weapons* should be secured and handled only by the assigned persons. Never assign a weapon to an actor whose mental stability or level of sobriety might be in question. It is very tempting for the young-at-heart and feeble-minded to play with weapons. This cannot be ignored or allowed. Put your foot down to the director and cast. Demand safe regulations, especially with firearms. The theatre industry has a long list of injuries and deaths due to accident, carelessness, and outright stupidity. Include in your list of guidelines at least the following:

■ Treat all firearms as if they are loaded and dangerous.

■ Never horse around.

■ Never allow weapons to lie around. They should be under lock and key whenever they are not in use. Even during performances, they should not be placed on prop tables where a stray audience member might find them.

A child from the audience, looking for a restroom, found instead an unattended prop table in the hall beside the stage. He proceeded to pick up a blank-firing pistol and pull the trigger. Luckily, he and the actors and the crews and the audience were merely startled half to death.

—DORIS SCHNEIDER

- Always check a gun to see if it is loaded.
- Do not load a gun until you have to.
- Do not cock a gun until you are ready to fire.
- Keep the weapon pointed up.
- If you are using a slide-action rifle, keep the slide open until ready to fire (it cannot fire when open).
- If you are using a pump-action rifle, keep the pump open until ready to fire.
- When using a revolver, load at least one extra cylinder in case of a misfire and to prevent a "click" when firing an empty chamber.
- If a gun does not fire on the first try (misfires), cock the hammer back and try it a second time. If it still does not fire, put it down facing away from anyone. Go to an alternative plan which should be worked out in rehearsal with the fight director. Get the gun offstage at the first opportunity. Do not fight with a gun that has misfired. Remember that it is still loaded and may go off accidentally. The gun must be unloaded by a qualified person.
- Know how many bullets a gun will hold. When unloading, check all cylinders of a revolver and remove the clip from a semiautomatic. Then check the chamber for a bullet which has been positioned for firing. Forgetting to check the firing chamber has caused many deaths.
- Practice shooting guns to eliminate fear and loss of control.
- Use appropriate cleaning procedures and cleaning tools for each type of firearm and clean after each use.
- Practice shooting inside the theatre to test for volume. An explosion that is too loud can be unnerving to an audience. Remember that sound is different in an empty theatre than in a full one.
- All ammunition must be protected from sudden impact or shock.
- If you are unsure about a weapon or a procedure, ASK!

5. Fire safety equipment, extinguishers, and first-aid kits need to be available and properly positioned.

COMBAT NOTATIONS

Combat for the stage is usually divided into two types: armed and unarmed. There is no standard system for notating stage combat; however, there are several fight masters who have written books on armed combat for the stage and have included systems with formats and symbols for notating fight sequences. William Hobbs and Arthur Wise are among the best known of these fight directors/authors. Their symbols represent terms unique to movements and to weapons used in *armed combat*. This text holds the first published notation system for *unarmed stage combat*. J. D. Martinez's book, *Combat Mime*, was used as a guideline in developing the notation system for unarmed combat. *Combat Mime* includes a well-organized written text accompanied by clear, easy-to-follow illustrations by Caren Caraway (see Figure 5-1). Martinez's formats for narrating and outlining fight sequences are incorporated in the Schneider Notation System and demonstrated in this chapter. *Combat Mime* is an excellent reference for learning terminology, techniques, and illusions employed in unarmed stage combat.

Fight directors often have their own individually developed system for notating combat. In working with a fight director, you should first ask about his/her method of notating. You may be provided with a written narration of each fight sequence; you may be given an outline with arrows and columns to indicate and separate aggressors and victims; or you may have to do all notating yourself. This is sometimes good.

You may use the fight director's system or transcribe his/her notes into the Schneider Notation System. Use the format which allows you to most easily notate fight sequences during rehearsals. Chapter 4 includes symbols for movement, direction, position, gesture, and anatomy. This chapter includes symbols for the most commonly used terms in unarmed stage combat.

FIGURE 5.1

NOTATIONS FOR UNARMED STAGE COMBAT

The purpose of notating stage combat is the same as that of notating stage move-ment: to provide an accurate readable record of a production; to provide infor-mation necessary for running rehearsals and performances; and to maintain the integrity of the original blocking/choreography. In stage combat, it is even more important that the notations be specific and complete because of the po-tential dangers inherent in the action and, subsequently, because of questions of liability. Therefore, in addition to accurate notations, a videotape of each se-quence is desirable but is not a substitute for complete and concise notations.

Each fight sequence should be notated in three parts: a *narrative,* an *out-line* and *stage pictures,* using words, symbols and special formatting.

NARRATIVE

The narrative may give a complete description of the fight or just a story line. If it is not provided by the fight director, the SM will need to write a narration following the combat blocking rehearsal. Even if the fight director furnishes the narration, the sequence may be lengthened, shortened, or completely changed during blocking rehearsals. It should be typed and inserted into the produc-tion book for reference. If six combatants are paired off and three different fight sequences are performed simultaneously, then three narrations are needed. The narration should be divided into steps or beats and numbered.

Example: Story-line narrative

Abe advances on Bob, shoves him down and contemptuously walks away. Bob gets up, follows and grabs Abe from behind, choking him. They struggle together until Abe breaks loose. Abe punches Bob who is surprised by the first punch but ducks the second one and retaliates with a kick to the groin. After a light shove, the injured and groaning Abe falls and Bob exits.

Example: Descriptive narrative

1. **A** walks up and with both hands shoves **B**. **B** stumbles backwards and falls to the ground from the force of the shove.

2. **A** contemptuously turns his back on **B** and begins to walk away. **B** rises from the floor, rushes upon the unsuspecting **A** and chokes **A** with a forearm from behind.

3. **A** and **B** are locked in a struggle, traveling across the stage, knocking a chair over.

4. **A** jabs **B** in the ribs with an elbow and **B** releases **A**.

5. **A** wheels around and, with a roundhouse, punches **B** in the face. **B** reels back-wards from the force of the blow.

6. **A** closes the distance and throws another roundhouse punch at **B**. Just in the nick of time, **B** ducks, avoiding the punch.

7. **B** immediately kicks **A** in the groin. **A** groans and crouches down in agony.

8. **B** contemptuously shoves **A** backwards and **A** falls to the ground. **B** then turns his back and walks away.

OUTLINE

The outline is a verbal/symbolic diagram of the fight. It gives only those details needed for the SM to follow the action of the fight. It should be made during
blocking. It should be written/drawn on the *Notation Graph* (see Chapter 4) in
the space provided for stage movement. The outline may separate characters
into columns which are divided into steps which correlate with the steps in
the narration. The examples in Figure 5-2 use words and standard abbreviations. Most of the words could be replaced by symbols.

Arrows may be used between the columns to identify the aggressor when
there are only two combatants. If there are three or more combatants, and one
is the victim, he/she can be identified with a circled V, instead of a character

FIGURE 5.2	SAMPLE SCRIPT BREAKDOWN

Combatant A (Abe)		Combatant B (Bob)
1. X slowly to B, 2 handed shove to chest	⟶	falls backwards
2. turns, X stage Right	⟵	rises, rushes to A, forearm choke from behind
3. both struggle backward, upstage Left, knocking chair over, ending in a full front position		
4. jabs B in ribs with elbow	⟶	contracts, releases A
5. circles B, roundhouse punch to face (knap)*	⟶	reels backward
6. follows B, roundhouse punch (misses)	⟶	ducks
7. contracts and groans	⟵	kicks A in groin (knap)*
8. falls	⟵	shoves A backwards turns and exits

*"Knap" refers to the sound made in stage combat (such as the sound of a slap, a kick,
or a punch). The knap may be made by the aggressor or the victim. It is important to
identify who makes the knap and to note it in the outline.

initial. It implies that his/her actions are all reactions to the aggressors, and saves time in notating and interpreting the notes.

A barroom brawl with multiple characters changing combat partners requires individual notation on common steps or beats. If combatants fight within smaller groups, you may notate each group separately. If words are used rather than symbols, several pages may be needed to complete the outline.

STAGE PICTURES

Stage pictures serve as a ground plan for fight sequences and should be drawn beside the outline to check blocking in rehearsals and performances. Types of combat movements cannot be shown on stage pictures, but use of space, rate

FIGURE 5.3	SAMPLE SCRIPT BREAKDOWN

Stage pictures

Combatant A (Abe)	Combatant B (Bob)
1. X slowly to B, 2 handed shove to chest	→ falls backwards
2. turns, X stage Right	← rises, rushes to A, forearm choke from behind
3. both struggle backward, upstage Left, knocking chair over, ending in a full front position	
4. jabs B in ribs with elbow →	contracts, releases A
5. circles B, roundhouse punch to face (knap)* →	reels backward
6. follows B, roundhouse punch (misses) →	ducks
7. contracts and groans	← kicks A in groin (knap)*

of movement, and character positions can be notated. Refer to Chapter 4 for instructions on drawing stage pictures. Well-drawn stage pictures are more quickly interpreted than linear writing of words or symbols. One picture should be drawn beside each step in the fight sequence unless that step includes no change in place or position. In Figure 5-3, note that there is no picture for Step 4.

Combat outlines and stage pictures should be inserted on the page facing any accompanying dialogue or appropriate script material, thus integrating fight sequences with other stage movement. The script may give only one line of description to represent a lengthy fight sequence. This makes it necessary to cut the script page and glue or copy the remaining dialogue on another sheet so there is sufficient space for the combat notations. Do not crowd notations because of script space. Instead, make the script fit notation needs. In order to run safe combat rehearsals, you must have clear readable notations.

UNARMED STAGE COMBAT SYMBOLS

Many of the symbols in Chapter 4 (especially the anatomy symbols) are also used in notating combat. Likewise, many of the combat symbols on the worksheet can be used in blocking noncombat scenes. Following the symbols are techniques and illusions described in *Combat Mime, A Non-Violent Approach to Stage Violence,* by J. D. Martinez.

THE SOCIETY OF
AMERICAN FIGHT DIRECTORS

The Society of American Fight Directors (SAFD) is a nonprofit organization which promotes the art of safe stage combat. Members of SAFD offer many levels of combat classes and workshops (including certification workshops) at major colleges, universities, and private schools across the country. The University of Neveda in Las Vegas hosts the National Stage Combat Workshops each summer for an intense three weeks of training. Membership is also open to "friends" who merely wish to receive *The Fight Master,* a journal that is published twice yearly and contains in-depth articles on the history and practice of stage combat, the latest equipment, and staging practices; and *The Cutting Edge,* a newsletter updating SAFD activities, policies, and member news.

For information, write or call:

Society of American Fight Directors
1834 Camp Avenue
Rockford, IL 61103
1-800-659-6579

Combat Symbols and Worksheet

Base symbols: contact · advance · fall · kick · punch · lunge · layout · knap · knife

Symbol							Symbol					
contact							chop					
non-contact							back-hand					
advance							round-house					
retreat							uppercut					
dodge							slap					
duck							scratch					
feint							bite					
side step L							choke					
side step R							cut					
block							smash					
contract							butt, head					
dive							butt, 2 heads					
roll							lunge					
fall							hold					
break-fall							struggle					
kick							release					
trip							layout					
stomp							knap					
punch							knife					
jab							gun					

TECHNIQUES AND ILLUSIONS

ROLLS:

Standard forward roll

Shoulder roll

Dive shoulder roll

Shoulder roll without hands

Aikido roll

FALLS:

Backward fall

Forward fall

Tripping

Side fall

Shoulder roll and layout

BREAKFALLS:

Judo side breakfall

Judo front breakfall

Judo back breakfall

CONTINUAL CONTACT TECHNIQUES:

Simple shoulder shove

Two hand chest shove

Face shove

Foot shove to stomach

Head throw into shoulder roll and layout

Push into a backward fall

Push over a bench into a side breakfall

Push from behind into a forward fall

Pulling clothing

Pulling hair, nose, ear

RESTRAINING:

    Bending arm behind back

    Choking, both hands from the front

    Choking, one hand from the front

    Forearm choke from behind

    Shove up against a wall

    Scratching, scratching the face

    Slap, double slap, triple slap

PUNCHING:

    Uppercut

    Roundhouse

    Jab

    Backhand punch

    Stomach punch

    Kidney punch

    Block and punch

    Elbow jab

    Cross jab 1

    Cross jab 2

    Hammer punch to the back

    Karate knife to the throat

KNEEING, KICKING, STOMPING:

    Knee in face

    Knee in groin

    Stomach kick

    Standing contact groin kick

    Rearend kick

    Foot stomp

    Stomping the stomach

    Knee drop to the back

ASSORTED THROWS, SMASHES, LIFTING, AND DRAGGING

Overhead foot throw to the side	
Hip throw	
Head throw	
Head smash against a table	
Head smash against a wall	WALL
Head butt	
Side fall (faint)	Sd
Cradle lift	CRADLE
Fireman's carry	FIREMAN'S
Underarm drag	
One wrist drag	1
Two wrist drag	2

NOTE: *Remember, a little knowledge is dangerous. The information in this chapter will make you more prepared to run stage combat rehearsals. However, it does not qualify you as fight captain, choreographer, or pyrotechnician. Prepare yourself further for managing stage combat by taking a course or workshop in stage combat in order to learn fight terminology and associate it with physical actions. Consider getting certified as a pyrotechnician. It will give your resumé a boost and may give you greater leverage in contract negotiations.*

STAGE MANAGING MUSICAL PERFORMANCES	6

There are many types of musical productions including musical plays, operettas, opera, and dance. They vary in the degree of dialogue and dance but they have many features in common such as an increased artistic staff, large casts, divided rehearsals, live music, more emphasis on spectacle, and specific health and safety concerns. These added complexities result in productions which are more difficult to stage manage both in rehearsal and performance.

Musicals are harder to stage manage than straight plays because there is a good deal going on at any given time, requiring a lot of cueing and backstage hustle and bustle. I prefer being busy that way. During some of the more quiet plays, you could raise a family between cues. There's something so deadly in that for a stage manager.

— BARRY KORNHAUSER, AEA STAGE MANAGER,
FULTON OPERA HOUSE

You do not need to be an accomplished dancer, singer, or musician to run rehearsals and call cues, but a basic knowledge of dance and the ability to read music will build confidence as well as competence. For opera, the ability to speak additional languages (especially Italian) provides a real advantage.

This chapter focuses on the particular needs of dancers and singers in auditions, rehearsals, and performances, and on the stage manager's role in answering those needs. The good news is that you can share some of the responsibilities with the specialized staff required for musical presentations. As with any company, the makeup and size of the staff will vary according to the budget of the company and the demands of the particular production.

The **artistic director** is the image maker (in charge of the realization of the mission of the company) and oversees the entire season of productions.

The Beggars Opera is staged at the Santa Fe Opera in 1992. The set designer was Paul Steinberg, lighting done by Craig Miller and direction given by Christopher Alden. (Photo © George Mott)

The *stage director* develops the vision of the individual production through collaboration with the artistic staff, interprets the script, and blocks the action.

The *music director/conductor* (usually but not always the same person) interprets the musical score, is in charge of all aspects of vocal and instrumental music and the meshing of the two, and conducts the **orchestra.** An *assistant conductor* replaces the conductor in an emergency, assists in rehearsals, and may cue the backstage chorus unless a mirror or monitor has been set up to allow the backstage chorus to see the conductor.

The **chorus master** (particularly in opera), using the conductor's interpretation, teaches the music to the **chorus** before they meet the conductor.

The *choreographer* creates dances and supervises all dance movement in a musical production. Like the fight director, the choreographer may be with the company only for as long as it takes to bring the dance numbers up to performance quality.

The *dance captain* is chosen by the choreographer. One of the dancers or an assistant stage manager with dance training may be appointed. The dance captain's tasks include teaching dance routines during auditions, leading in warm-ups prior to each rehearsal and performance, and maintaining the integrity of the original choreography.

The stage manager's role in musical productions grows with the size of the staff. With so many contributing artists, the rarified theatre air can become charged with creative energy or destructive tension. The SM's role is one of diplomacy in anticipating and resolving conflicts by facilitating communication and collaboration.

AUDITIONS

Prior to auditions, you must secure a space (or spaces) appropriate for the types of auditions to be held. For a musical play, you may need several audition rooms: one for acting, one for singing, and one for dance. This allows two or more auditions to occur simultaneously. The audition space, as well as rehearsal space, for dance ideally should be a large open room with a *sprung floor* (a wooden floor built on joists to give it resilience). A sprung floor can move (give) with the weight of a dancer, especially in leaps and jumps. Avoid using a concrete floor. Equity contracts prohibit the use of concrete or marble floors or any other surface deemed injurious or unsafe. Check the floor for splinters, holes, or protrusions such as raised nails, screws, or staples. If possible, cover the floor with a *dance floor* (for more details, see p. 169).

A waiting room for the actors and a warm-up room for dancers and singers are desirable. For dancers, the audition room and warm-up room should be similar in temperature, at least seventy degrees, and preferably higher. For singers, adequate warmth, moist air, and drinking water with paper cups are desirable.

Do all preparatory paper work required for regular auditions so all participants are well informed (see Chapter 2).

Arrange for an accompanist and a piano or keyboard and/or tape deck in the singing and dancing audition spaces.

Acting auditions are the same as in a nonmusical play (see Chapter 2).

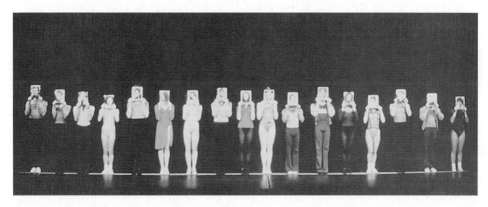

A chorus line of dancers present their talents in an "audition" during a production of the musical *A Chorus Line.* (Photo by Martha Swope © Time Inc.)

Singing auditions for musical plays require organization and control of the flow of singers and maintenance of paperwork (audition forms, resumés, etc.).

Dance auditions require you to free the choreographer and dance captain from any responsibilities besides concentrating on the auditions. The dance captain will teach a routine while the choreographer observes their skills and ability to learn the steps. You and your staff will take notes, start and stop tapes of music, and manage people. If singing and acting auditions are going on simultaneously with dance, you can assign the above tasks to an ASM while you coordinate and oversee the auditions.

There are often large numbers of dancers auditioning for roles. Consult with the choreographer for any preferred method of moving groups or individuals in for auditions. One method for identifying dancers and establishing order is to give out numbered cards on which each person will write their name, height, hair color, sex, and colors or identifying characteristics of clothing. Collect the cards, organize them into groups, and give the cards to the choreographer. This allows you to call groups of dancers in by numbers and helps the choreographer identify each dancer. You may also choose to have a correlating number on an adhesive-backed card attached to the front of each dancer's garment. The play/movie *A Chorus Line* demonstrates the elimination process of chorus auditions. The choreographer selects dancers from each group, forming new groups as the dance captain leads them in combinations which become more and more complex. Eventually, one group remains and from it the chorus line is chosen. Rejection is painful, but as soon as a dancer is dismissed, move him/her out of the space to allow concentration of the remaining dancers and an unbroken flow of auditions.

Opera auditions rarely require the presence of the stage manager. At the Metropolitan Opera House, which has a different production each day of the week, there is a staff for auditioning. There is a stage manager for each different opera, and while one opera is in performance, others are being rehearsed. At smaller opera houses, the principals are often auditioned in another city while the chorus is auditioned locally. The stage manager may be expected to help with the chorus audition.

PRODUCTION MEETINGS

The *stage director, music director* and *choreographer* collaborate on characterization and mood in songs and dances. Note this information. You may need it in maintaining the integrity of the production later, especially if the dance captain is one of the dancers and cannot observe the dance from an objective position. The music director and stage director should discuss any music that demands that the singer be in a position which limits projection (such as reclining, behind scenery, etc.).

The *choreographer* should attend early production meetings to collaborate with the artistic staff about costume, prop, and scenery needs for safe rehearsals and performances. If the choreographer is not present, you must ensure those needs are met. Take notes on everything.

Set designs for musical plays usually allow a lot of floor space for large casts (choruses) and dance. Construction, material, and surface condition of the floor is the most important consideration to plan for in rehearsal and performance. A sprung floor is not always available for dancers and the surface of the floor may be unacceptable. However, a permanent or nonpermanent floor covering can improve an otherwise unsafe floor. Battleship linoleum is a good permanent surface for dance. A thin vinyl nonpermanent flooring is sold specifically for dance and can be ordered from theatrical supply companies. It comes in rolls which can be laid out and taped to the stage floor and taped at seams where pieces of vinyl meet. Request tape which has the same color and surface as the vinyl. Ballet dancers can slip on slick tape and modern dancers cannot slide their feet across rough tape.

Scenery that is to be integrated into the musical numbers must be evaluated for safety, sound effects, and stability. For example, platforms and stairs that will hold large choruses or will be danced on should be built with extra supports. A staircase, which a soloist must descend while singing, should have risers and treads of a height and depth which are safe and allow the performer to concentrate on the music rather than the action.

Platform surfaces (like floor surfaces) are of significance to dancers and should be planned according to their use. Tap dancing requires sound, so a hard surface such as wood or masonite is desired. If the platform is upstage, you may need to bring in the sound designer to mike the floor in order to pick up the tapping. Modern dance requires a surface which mutes sound and is safe for bare feet. A piece of dance floor cut to fit the platform is best but muslin over padding is also good. If the dancers will be on pointe and spinning, however, a muslin-covered platform would not be appropriate. For safety, it is desirable to have all platforms and stairs available for rehearsal at least two weeks before performance.

Props used in musical productions should be available early in rehearsal as their use must be carefully timed and coordinated with the music and movement. Set deadlines and see that they are communicated to all persons involved in fulfilling them. If your production is *The Mikado* and you need fifteen Japanese fans for the chorus, you should request extras (even for rehearsal). Some will disappear; some may be damaged (depending on the way they are used). The same advice is appropriate for canes, umbrellas, hats, or any other prop or costume piece that can be easily damaged due to its construction or use. Request a lockable space to hold rehearsal props and costumes, preferably in or near the rehearsal hall.

Costume designs should be evaluated for freedom of movement and use of voice. Any costume piece that might interfere with singing (such as a mask or a tight bodice) should be evaluated and modified. Any costume pieces that a

Members of the internationally acclaimed African-American Dance Ensemble show their unique style of dance. Founder and artistic director for the ensemble is Chuck Davis. (Photo by Rebecca Lesher)

dancer must become accustomed to moving in (such as bustles, hoops, long skirts, or robes) and anything that becomes part of the choreography (such as hats or capes) must be listed for rehearsal use, and deadlines must be set for their availability.

Special effects such as fog or smoke should be discussed in terms of health and safety. Any airborne particles might affect a singer's voice. Also, some special effects (such as fog) can create a slippery floor, which is dangerous for dancers. Schedule a time to test these effects and have alternative plans in case they prove to be a problem.

Rehearsal music will be determined by the music director and choreographer. Piano is often used for ballet, but taped music is preferred by many because it is consistent–the timing never changes. However, it must match the timing of the music used in the show. If a tape is to be used, schedule the taping and procure a tape deck for rehearsals.

Lighting effects will be discussed by the lighting designer and choreographer. Special lighting effects that might affect safety and concentration (such as very dim lights, strobe lights, etc.), should be in use as soon as is practical in order for the performers to adjust to them.

Sound effects that might affect timing in singing and dance should be discussed and scheduled for availability early in rehearsals. Also, the sound designer should plan with the music director on the miking of the stage. A young cast may need personal mikes to project above the orchestra. A mature cast will only need mikes placed in strategic positions on or above the stage.

REHEARSALS AND PERFORMANCES

The stage manager's responsibilities for rehearsals and performances of music and dance are basically the same as in any theatrical production. All aspects of scheduling, organizing, running rehearsals and performances, trouble-shooting, and maintaining the production family should be overseen if not personally accomplished.

For example, the responsibility of rehearsing dance and maintaining the integrity of the choreography is usually left to the dance captain, not the SM. However, you or an ASM should be at all rehearsals. You are a liaison between the stage director and the choreographer, although you may not have much input unless there are behavioral problems that affect the ability of individuals to maintain the show and the sense of family, especially during a long run.

For singers, sweeping the stage and checking the floor surface for safety is not enough. You should also damp mop the floor and mist with water to eliminate floating dust particles and provide some moisture to an otherwise arid atmosphere, which is hard on a singer's voice. Arrange for water stations and disposable drinking cups on both sides of the stage.

Warm-ups for singers may be done as a chorus. Soloists often prefer to warm up alone because there are many approaches to vocal training that have individualized warm-up techniques.

Warm-ups for dancers are lead by the dance captain, or he/she may assign the task to various dancers to keep it fresh. Some dancers do individual warm-ups in their dressing rooms rather than group warm-ups. However, many directors require participation in group warm-ups because they can use this time to give out information.

Rehearsals for music, dance, and scene work are often held simultaneously in different spaces. Eventually the calls are combined to coordinate the three.

> *In opera, the conductor works with the singers just on music for a very short time. Then the stage director takes over for the bulk of the rehearsals. The conductor attends rehearsals and can make music interjections or give notes or schedule private rehearsals as needed to maintain the music.*
>
> —MARIE MERKEL, FREELANCE PRODUCTION STAGE MANAGER FOR OPERA

All performers want to work in a hazard-free healthy environment. Singers are especially concerned about clean air and temperature control. A cold or an irritated throat can compromise or even eliminate a singer's voice. Likewise, dancers require warm rehearsal spaces to help prevent muscle injury. An actor can give lines with a hoarse voice and may even be able to perform a role in a leg cast, but singers and dancers do not have such flexibility. Therefore, in a musical production, it is desirable to have a doctor on call.

This is often a voluntary service by a board member. At the Metropolitan Opera House, there is a doctor in the house every night and a nurse on duty every day. As stage manager, you should stock up on cough drops, tea, honey, bottled water, ice packs, and elastic bandages.

Another unique aspect of stage managing musical productions is working with an orchestra. You or the production manager may be responsible for having instruments tuned. If you are working with musicians paid by the hour, you may deal with a liaison for the orchestra who synchronizes watches with you to monitor rehearsal and performance times. The issue ultimately is budget.

Specifics for rehearsing singers vary according to the type of performance. In opera, very demanding roles are sometimes double cast because the principal cannot sing two days in a row. This means extra rehearsals. Principals are usually professionals and rehearse during the day. The chorus may be made up of singers with other jobs and therefore must rehearse in the evenings. They can then be put together on weekends and some evenings. The **supernumeraries** (extras, called "supers"), who have no speaking or singing roles, also come in the evenings. The stage director works with them and often has the ASM walk the roles of the principals in early rehearsals. The principals are then plugged in at a later date.

Operas are usually on a tight schedule and the principals may come already knowing their lyrics. It is difficult to give line notes unless you speak the language. Otherwise, you must assign someone who speaks the language to keep the notes. If there are supertitles (lines on a screen above the stage), the words must be faithful–especially if the opera is in English.

Opera is 100 percent musically cued, so the stage manager must be able to read music in order to follow the score and to call the show.

Stage managing opera is a challenge–similar to a three ring circus because you have so many elements coming together with huge casts that sometimes include children and animals. But, when things get tense, I listen to the music and I realize–that's what it's all about.

—MARIE MERKEL, FREELANCE PRODUCTION STAGE MANAGER FOR OPERA

What's unique about stage managing at the Met? That's easy. Every day I am surrounded by the most beautiful music in the world.

—THOMAS CONNELL, AGMA PRODUCTION STAGE MANAGER,
METROPOLITAN OPERA HOUSE

Specifics for rehearsing dancers in a musical play are primarily centered around safety considerations but also include a few practical suggestions. The rehearsal floor should be taped so the dancers will know where **center stage,** scenery, entrances, exits, and the front edge of the stage is. The choreographer may also ask you to tape the front of the stage or the plaster line (front edge of the **proscenium opening**) with marks representing one foot measurements

Production stage manager Thomas Connell is on stage during the final dress rehearsal of the 1996 production of *Falstaff* at the Metropolitan Opera House. (Photo by Winnie Klotz)

from the center line (see Figure 6-1). These marks will help him/her plan positions and help the dancers maintain them.

If an open **orchestra pit** is being used, you may also need to put down glow tape to prevent a fall from the edge of the stage. This is a greater concern

FIGURE 6.1

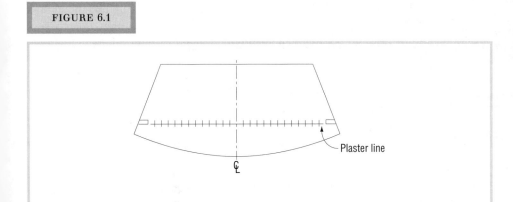

Plaster line

when **spotlights** are used and the dancers' vision beyond the pool of light is impaired. It is also important to keep an unused pit cleared of chairs, music stands and other objects which could turn a bad fall into a disaster.

The amount of time needed for dance rehearsal depends on the number in the chorus and their level of skill. If a chorus is large, you may have assistants to the dance captain to help teach choreography and keep everybody on track. You may have to adjust rehearsal time for learning choreography. Some dancers will learn quickly, while others will require extra time with the dance captain. If you observe errors being made in a dance rehearsal, as stage manager, normally you would not stop the dance, but would let the dance captain make that decision.

If the errors become a major train wreck—not even close to the original choreography—stop them! If the mistake is something they can pick up later and you just want to keep the flow going, let them finish the dance. You may observe that the same one or two people are always off, causing the eventual train wreck. But if they're all starting at the wrong place, you may need to stop the dance and correct the problem. Again, most of these decisions can be left to the dance captain. However, this does not release you from following the dance. The dance captain may be one of the dancers and may ask you, "Where did everybody get off?"

—WILLIAM C. BROWN, FREELANCE STAGE MANAGER
AND LIGHTING DESIGNER

Music for dance rehearsals is usually taped and you or one of your staff will operate the tape deck. It is desirable to have the music director accompany rehearsals for two weeks before the show. You may not have the full orchestra more than two or three rehearsals before opening. Budget and schedule conflicts are the main factors.

Costumes for dancers require more repair and laundry because there is more potential for them to rip and to be soiled by perspiration. Be sure there is a dresser or costume running crew carrying out this maintenance. Dancers often have quick costume changes, requiring a space backstage and assistance from a dresser. Props often have to be handed to or taken from dancers as they dance on or off stage. Be sure someone is assigned this task.

In the Ice Capades, *there are buckets ready to take parasols because the skaters are spinning around going back to pick something else up. You have to be creative about how to collect and dispense props quickly. Sometimes the entire running crew may be needed to hand out costume pieces or props rather than having a huge costume or prop crew for that one scene.*

—WILLIAM C. BROWN, FREELANCE STAGE MANAGER
AND LIGHTING DESIGNER

> *NOTE: Be sure all entrances and exits are clear for dancers as they must keep their specified pace and may be leaping, backing up, or executing some other movement that does not allow them to dodge people or objects in their way. Side lights and cables for these lights are a particular problem. Tape the cables to the floor so a foot cannot get caught, and show the performers where the cables are laid so they will not stumble over the unavoidable protrusion.*

Lights are something dancers must learn to work with because they will be in their eyes at all times. In addition to front and back lighting, side lights are used to give extra illumination to the dancers' bodies and movements. Dancers must learn to focus out of the lights (look in the spaces between lights or look at the floor without looking down). For this reason, young dancers need more rehearsal time with lights than seasoned dancers.

Moving from a bright stage to dark wings or moving from bright light to a blackout causes temporary blindness. Also, spinning (which can be choreographed into any style of dance) can cause a temporary loss of orientation. The solution to each of the above problems is "spotting lights." A red light or something that can be seen easily by the dancer should be placed at the back of the **house** (audience seating area) or in the booth so that the turning or spinning dancer knows where he/she is. Spotting lights strategically placed in the wings can provide the guidance needed for exits. Another solution for helping blinded dancers/actors off during a blackout is to have someone go on stage and get them. Glow tape can be used to guide a performer's steps, but too much is distracting to the audience. You do not want the stage to light up during a blackout. It breaks the magic spell. Glow tape is very helpful on exit stairs, however, as well as behind scenery, or upstage of furniture or other set props where the audience cannot see it.

Follow spots are also hard on dancers' eyes. The rule is if it is going to be difficult to work with, begin working with it early. Some directors do not want lights early. They consider them distracting to their directing. Others would give their eye teeth to have them early. However, if the light crew is being paid by the rehearsal or by the hour, that poses another problem. You or one of your staff may be able to bring in the stage lights early even if they are not cued correctly just so the dancers can get used to them.

Technical cues for dances must be synchronized with the music and the movement. The ability to read music is helpful, but sometimes there is no music (in some very modern pieces, for example) requiring the SM to call cues based on visuals. Some SM's prefer visual cues because a discrepancy in a dancer's timing or an accident or error on stage may require a change in cueing. In such an instance, it is better to be observing the performance than reading the music. Thus you need to attend enough dance rehearsals to at least be familiar with the use of stage space and any visual cues that will be important in calling the show.

In some companies, performers (rather than the conductor) can control the pace of the show. You must stay alert to changes in pace which will affect the timing of your cues. Some scripts allow improvisation or spontaneous interaction with the audience (especially children's plays or very modern dance productions). Chuck Davis, founder and choreographer for the African-American Dance Ensemble, has a dynamic personality and often, without warning, will change the order of a performance to involve the audience. The freshness and spontaneity resulting from his style of performance has made the company very popular. One of his stage managers, William C. Brown (an important contributor to this chapter), said he has to anticipate change, be ready to make quick decisions, and prepare his crew for the same.

Safety is an ongoing concern. Look for hazards in the rehearsal and performance spaces and think in terms of prevention of accidents. Is the floor safe? Is the temperature correct? Are the wings cleared? Although the floor may have an appropriate surface, what is its condition? A wet floor may need to be dried, a slippery floor may need rosin, and so on. If an accident occurs, have emergency numbers ready to be called to summon care for the injured. In the interim, you must provide necessary aid and comfort. All stage managers should be trained in first aid and CPR.

If an injury occurs *during a rehearsal,* the obvious response is to stop rehearsal and care for the victim. You can then continue the rehearsal without the dancer or use the opportunity to rehearse an understudy. Some dancers want to go on no matter what, and are willing to risk further injury. They must be stopped. Other dancers will call every minor injury so they can stop. They may be too cautious and their delays may affect performance quality or the ability to make the show happen. Once again, the SM must be the instrument of balance.

If a serious injury occurs *during a performance,* you have to decide whether to:

- allow the dancer to continue and risk increasing the injury;
- send in an understudy;
- continue without the dancer, making the absence as inconspicuous as possible;
- or (if there is no understudy and the victim is a lead character) stop the show.

This is not an easy decision and many factors should be considered in making it. Is the show near the beginning or the end? Can you take an unscheduled act break, giving the dancer time to rest, and giving you time to get emergency medical treatment or time simply to observe the injury? Sometimes you can tell about the severity of the injury through some simple triage. The amount of pain a performer is experiencing can often be read in his/her body language. For more information on first-response care to common dance injuries, see Chapter 7. A wrapped ankle or knee, which has a minor sprain, might get the show through a final scene.

NOTATIONS FOR DANCE

There are two well-known notation systems for dance—Laban and Benesh. They are very thorough and complex and too detailed to use during a blocking rehearsal or for calling cues. The main purpose of these systems is to document the choreography. If you are stage managing for a professional dance company, your dance captain may be able to carry out this task for the choreographer.

As a stage manager for a musical play, your notation responsibilities are limited due to time and purpose. Blocking rehearsals usually only allow time for notating the use of stage space: entrances, exits, coupling, starting positions, major movement segments, who is on a line and where, and so on. Most of this can be done with stage pictures. The purpose of your notations is to allow you to call technical cues and to have an overall sense of the order and movement of the dance. The dance captain, not you, is responsible for the integrity of the choreography. If, however, you know dance well enough, you may have much input in maintaining dances.

Scripts for musical plays may include lyrics but do not usually include the musical score. Follow the guidelines in Chapter 4 for transferring a script to the notation format and insert the sheet music where it should be in the script. You may have to reduce the size of the music to fit the script space on the notation format (see Figure 6-2 on the next page).

On the pages facing the music, copy as many stage diagrams or shapes representing the stage as you anticipate needing. These stage drawings may be blank or they may be drawn with the traditional divisions of stage geography (see Figure 6-3).

FIGURE 6.3	SAMPLE USING TRADITIONAL STAGE GEOGRAPHY

FIGURE 6.2

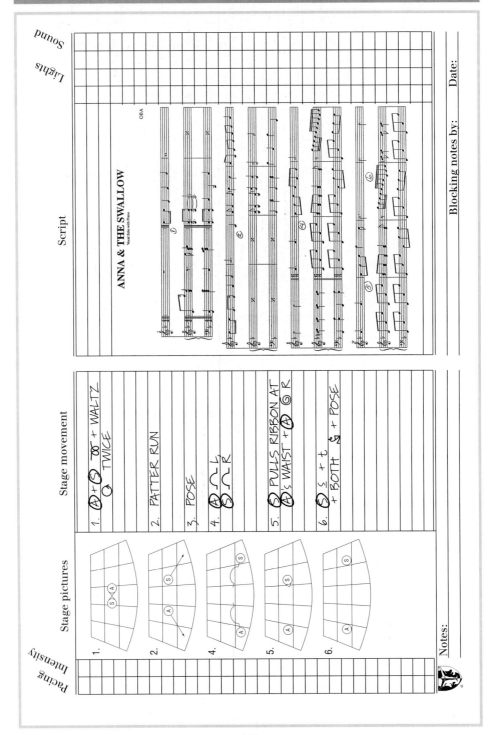

The divisions can assist in drawing stage pictures with accurate patterns of movement. Correlate the stage pictures with the music, lyrics, or visual cues written in the script (see Figure 6-2).

> *NOTE: It is not necessary to write in the dance steps, only the use of stage space, but if you know dance terminology and can notate it, do so. It can be only an advantage, especially in rehearsing understudies or replacement dancers.*

Alternate formating can be used to accommodate the type of dance and number of dancers involved (see Figure 6-4). You may need more spaces for stage pictures, requiring the full page facing the music.

Stage managing musical plays is extremely demanding and stressful. Additional chiefs (choreographer, music director, choral director) and their assistants compete for your attention in this creative tribe. Additional scenery, lighting cues, special effects, and simultaneous rehearsals further complicate an already difficult job. Insist on a stage management staff adequate to shoulder most of the traditional responsibilities so you can focus on communication and coordination. Since you are filling the role, request that you are billed as the Production Stage Manager. It may not change your pay level but it might improve treatment and respect from peers, and it will enhance your resumé.

FIGURE 6.4 | SAMPLE USING ONLY THE CENTERLINE TO DEFINE SPACE

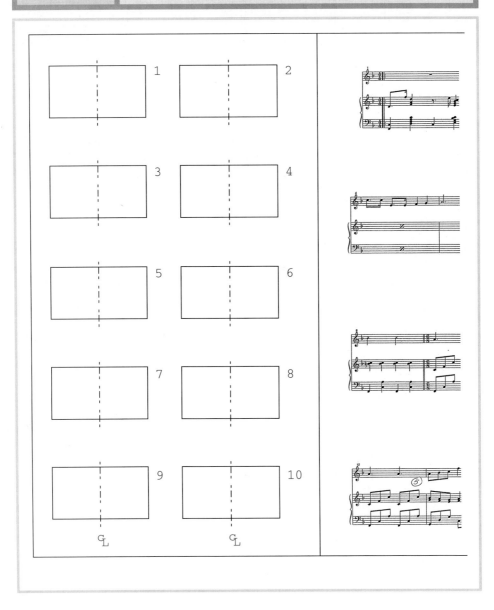

HEALTH AND SAFETY GUIDES

7

The theatre is a place and an occupation fraught with hazard. Injury, illness, and death linger on stage, wait in the wings, and boldly stalk the shops and even the dressing rooms. Due to a lack of time, personnel, and budget, the laws and organizations that were created to protect all American employees are too often ignored in the theatre or in the control of products made for the theatre. Artists, like lovers, can seduce themselves into believing that passion provides some kind of divine protection from the results of carelessness or even recklessness.

Newspapers and tabloids commonly report deaths due to errors in occupations that involve few tools and procedures and are governed by strict regulations. How much more dangerous is the theatre where students and volunteers with minimal experience sometimes greatly outnumber knowledgable practitioners and are expected to participate in projects which can involve electrical wiring, welding, power tools, firearms, explosives, hazardous chemicals, lifting and climbing, and experimentation? These are just the crew tasks, done simply for the sake of illusion. What about the equal or even greater risks that we ask of actors? Unfortunately, most often these activities are carried out in too little time, under too much stress, and with too much love to notice the danger.

The guidelines and information in this chapter will help you recognize hazards and exercise the ounce of prevention that is worth a pound of the cure. These guidelines will prepare you to respond to some emergencies, but they do not cover all safety considerations in the production of a play, nor do they replace the need for a good first-aid course. No text can predict all of the hazards and accidents that might occur in the theatre or provide the hands-on training and experience needed for CPR administration or other emergency medical procedures. The rule of theatre is "expect the unexpected." This

J. B. Alston, technical director and photographer, strikes a piece of high scenery. Two crew members anchor the ladder by standing on either side.

chapter focuses only on those production phases that are supervised or assisted by the stage manager.

At the Metropolitan Opera House, where there is always a doctor in the audience and a nurse on staff, stage management health and safety responsibilities are very specific. The stage manager is the "public voice," executing decisions made with the help of the administrative staff, the management staff, and security.

> *There have been many emergencies in my years at the Met. They range from tear-gassings, to bomb scares (both political), to a suicide leap from the balcony into the orchestra pit, to a heart attack in the center orchestra seating area. They were all show-stoppers. In each such emergency, I make an announcement from the stage to calmly clear the auditorium so the emergency teams can do their jobs.*
>
> —THOMAS CONNELL, AGMA PRODUCTION STAGE MANAGER,
> METROPOLITAN OPERA HOUSE

In an educational theatre, the director, technical director, and other supervisors are expected to oversee the use of safety practices by the cast and crews. However, during a performance, the stage manager may be the highest ranking person aware of an emergency, and he/she must be prepared to respond.

Even the professional stage manager's job description probably will not include responsibility for the safety and health of the cast and backstage crews. Nevertheless, as the stage manager/primary caregiver, it will probably be *expected* of you.

You cannot be everywhere, monitoring each aspect of production. However, with a few guidelines (some of which are required by law), you can initiate or assist in a reasonable plan for protecting the rights and health of each individual while protecting your own liability.

In addition to interviews with fight directors and pyrotechnics, there are several very good published sources which were used for much of the information in this chapter. They are each excellent references covering a broad perspective on theatre safety and are wonderful tools for theatre-safety training programs.

Stage Fright, Health and Safety in the Theatre, by Monona Rossol. Allworth Press: New York, 1991.

Play It Safe, Introduction to Theatre Safety (video), narrated by David Fenner. Theatre Arts Video Library, Leucadia, CA, 1994.

The Pocket Guide to Theatre Safety, by Dr. Randall W. A. Davidson and Paul Vierra. Risk International, Inc., Campbell, CA, 1990.

Firearm Safety Onstage (video), with Robert B. Chambers. Theatre Arts Video Library, Leucadia, CA, 1992.

THE LAW AND LIABILITY

There are many regulations, laws, ordinances, and codes that should define your theatre's safety procedures. Maintain an up-to-date file on federal, state, and municipal guidelines, particularly those related to fire safety, building and construction codes, sanitation standards, environmental protection, and hazardous materials. It can make a difference in liability for death or injury by negligence, conviction of which can lead to prison as well as financial devastation.

Laws such as the Occupational Safety and Health Act (OSHA) have been formed to protect workers. OSHA has set legally enforceable minimum standards for workplace safety and health. Contact your nearest OSHA office (under U.S. Department of Labor) for a copy of the *General Industry Standards* booklet that applies to theatres and shops.

Liability laws vary with the state and responsibility for implementing safety programs; compliance with the laws varies with the company. Just as OSHA regulations are meant to protect the employee from harm, a consciencious adherence to these regulations should protect the employer from liability suits. As stage manager you are not the employer, but you may be assigned to represent the employer in enforcing safety regulations during rehearsals and performances. This means you must understand the regulations, follow them, and document everything not in compliance with them.

One of the newer regulations is especially important to theatre because of the varied materials used in the shop and onstage. They are called "right to know" laws which have been passed by some states and by the federal regulation called the OSHA Hazard Communication Standard. Violations of these regulations can lead to citations and steep fines as well as a requirement of immediate compliance with the law or a closing of your theatre.

The regulations include the following:

- Inventory all workplace chemicals, regardless of how harmless you think they are.
- Identify all hazardous products on your inventory list and mark them as such.
- Request Material Safety Data Sheets (MSDSs) from manufacturers or distributors for all products in inventory.
- Relabel or dispose of any products that have improper or incomplete labels.
- Identify procedures that use hazardous products or that can cause a product to become hazardous.
- Post or make available to personnel all written materials concerning hazardous products used in your environment.
- Train all personnel in the safe use of equipment and products.

Do not shrug these regulations off as being strictly applicable to technical directors and their scene shops. Hazardous chemicals are used onstage and in the dressing rooms, affecting the health of actors, backstage crews, and even the audience.

SAFETY STEPS

The following guidelines are based on research, personal experience, and common sense. Although this represents an attempt at generic guidelines, it must be remembered that each theatre, shop, company, and production is unique in its hazard producing as well as hazard reducing capabilities.

This is my favorite story . . . you probably can't use it [wrong—it is now my favorite story also] *but I'll tell you anyway. In the rehearsal of 1969 (a very active show), two women walked towards each other, carrying chairs which they were supposed to whip around and sit in. One night, one of the*

*women hit her head on the back of the chair. I stopped rehearsal. She
was conscious but wanted to lie still for a while and didn't want people
hovering around her. I had been bringing my dog to rehearsals, expecting
him to be worked into the show, so I called him and he lay beside her,
administering canine therapy. Whenever I see that actress, she reminds me
of the incident and how effective that therapy was. It helped her to feel
calm and quiet but not abandoned or isolated.*

—CRAIG WEINDLING, AEA STAGE MANAGER

So, consider the following recommendations for health protection and accident prevention and adapt them to your particular company. Like Chapter 2,
the guidelines are organized according to the production process. However,
that does not mean you should put off dealing with a known hazard until you
reach that phase of the rehearsal or production process.

PREPRODUCTION

1. Establish with the director or producer exactly what your responsibilities
    are in the administration of health and safety procedures. Get definite in-
    formation about your liability and the company's liability insurance. If
    necessary, get it in writing.

2. Determine what health and safety procedures are already in place, their
    adequacy, and how they are enforced. One way to develop and enforce
    procedures is to create a health and safety committee composed of at least
    one member of each division of the production company (lighting, cos-
    tuming, construction, cast, staff, makeup, etc.). These individuals can as-
    sist in the training and supervision of the safe use of tools and materials in
    their work places as well as anticipate potential problems and assist in re-
    solving them.

3. Evaluate and become familiar with your audition, rehearsal, and perfor-
    mance spaces. Inspect each of these spaces for safety hazards early enough
    in the schedule to allow time for improvement or a change of location if
    necessary. Develop strategies for working safely in unchangeable loca-
    tions and put your strategies as well as your concerns in writing to give to
    the producer. Add to the following checklist according to the construction
    and use of the space:

    - Locate the master switch for controlling all electrical current.
    - Check for first-aid kits and fire extinguishers.
    - Get information on the working condition and operation of fire alarms
      and built-in fire controls such as **fire curtains** or sprinkler systems.
    - Check the condition of and procedure for controlling the heating, cool-
      ing, and ventilating systems.

- Check the restrooms for convenience and sanitation and check for safe drinking water.
- Look for faulty wiring, poor floor conditions, and any other hazards that might cause injury or delay rehearsals or performances.
- Locate emergency exits and make sure they are not blocked.
- Post emergency numbers and procedures for emergency evacuation at a central location.
- Procure keys needed for entrances, emergency exits, and security.
- Arrange for corrections of any problems located in the above list.

4. At the first all-staff production meeting, collaborate with the director, choreographer, fight director, technical director, and each designer about safety procedures and concerns. Include any questions about unusual scenery, platforming, lighting, costumes, choreography, blocking, special effects, pyrotechnics, or use of firearms that wave a hazard sign from the script or the drawing boards. For example, a fencing scene on a narrow staircase without a hand rail, a running mob scene with strobe lighting, a chase scene in billowing period costumes through a set busy with fragile furniture and breakable knick-knacks, or a blindfolded actor running downstage are all potential accidents.

The blindfolded actor, in a moment of enthusiasm, ran off the apron of the stage and landed on his head against the iron support of an audience seat. Big headache—no permanent damage.

—DORIS SCHNEIDER

AUDITIONS

1. Sweep the audition and warm-up room floors, looking for staples, nails, or splintering wood. If the floor condition is still unacceptable, lay down a portable dance floor.
2. Post audition instructions, underlining or highlighting those that specifically refer to safety. Post no-smoking signs where appropriate and enforce them.
3. If there is to be combat, acrobatics, or any other physical activity that requires a soft floor, provide mats and protective body gear (masks, pads, etc.). Check all weapons and gear for fight readiness. Have fighters warm up.
4. Be sure the warm-up room for dancers is just that—warm. A cold room can lead to muscle injuries.
5. Be alert to any activities which look like they might cause injury. For example, an overzealous fighter might take unusual risks in order to demonstrate skill and desire for a role.

ACTING REHEARSALS

1. Maintain both the rehearsal floor and an appropriate room temperature and ventilation.

2. Identify eating, smoking and nonsmoking areas and provide ashtrays where appropriate.

3. Arrange for a safety training session which should include at least the following:

   - A review of company safety regulations
   - Emergency procedures
   - Emergency evacuation route followed by a drill
   - Protective equipment (if needed)
   - An explanation of OSHA regulations and the right-to-know laws
   - Location of MSDSs and how to detect hazardous chemicals

   Ask cast and rehearsal crew members for information on any medical conditions (such as epilepsy, allergies, or asthma) that might require emergency treatment, as well as their physicians' names and phone numbers, health insurance information, and medications in use that might impair their judgment or physical capabilities. Prepare a statement that verifies that they understand and will follow safety codes of the company and include a place for their signature and the date.

4. Collect rehearsal props, checking them for safe use. For example, if an actor is supposed to dance on a table, choose a sturdy one (the table, that is). If combat weapons are used, assign their care and handling to an ASM. If firearms are used, demonstrate the proper care, handling, and safety guidelines to the entire cast. If explosives or other pyrotechnical effects are used, station an ASM or PA with a fire extinguisher in a location as close to the hazard as possible.

5. During blocking rehearsals, be alert to any movements that might become hazardous once the platforming and scenery is in place.

6. Stop **horseplay**, especially with weapons, props, or anything that could become a weapon.

7. Keep wing space clear of props or people that can become a hazard to an exiting actor or dancer.

LOAD-IN AND SET-UP

1. Consult with the technical director about the order of the load-in (bringing the scenery and equipment from the truck or shop to the stage) and set-up (hanging and focusing lights, rigging and hanging scenery, setting up props, and arranging the prop tables and scene dock). Many activities

such as hanging lights or scenery and reweighting the **arbor** require silence and a minimum number of people on stage in order to hear warning calls. Plan the order of the load-in to accommodate these safety requirements.

2. Review safety procedures and rules as well as warning signals. Identify the master electrical switch and explain emergency treatment for shock victims. Point out the location(s) of first-aid kits and check the kits for proper contents.

3. Keep one spotter on smaller ladders to anchor them while in use and two spotters on either side of extension folding ladders.

4. Crew members' pockets, as well as the stage, should be empty when crews are working on the **grid.**

5. Place the scene dock (storage for scenery not in use) and prop tables out of the way of exiting actors.

6. Look for potential hazards backstage, especially in the stage exit areas.

An exiting dancer leaped from a platform (rather than walking down the escape steps) and crashed into a raised (but not high enough) roll-door. The remainder of the performance was spent in the emergency room with a head injury. The roll-door should have been padded and lighted. The dancer should have thought.

—DORIS SCHNEIDER

7. Tape or cover loose electrical cables on the floor to prevent tripping.

8. Arrange for adequate ventilation in the dressing rooms.

9. If fog or smoke is to be used, adjust the ventilation to prevent the movement of the heavy substance into the orchestra pit and audience. Some people are allergic to it; others just do not like it.

TECHNICAL REHEARSALS

1. Acquaint all running crew members with safety procedures and rules that apply to performances. Encourage calm and tolerance. Technical rehearsals are grueling and often lead to temper flare-ups, which can cause carelessness or health-threatening stress.

2. Horseplay is really *out.* So are alcohol and drugs.

3. If it has not already been done, collect emergency health information on crew members just as you did on the cast.

4. Check on the placement and working status of fire extinguishers, especially if pyrotechnics are to be used. Be sure you have the right type of ex-

tinguisher for potential fires. ABC extinguishers handle all types of fires. The important rule is to never use water on chemical or electrical fires.

5. If you have irregular or hazardous levels for performing on or routes for exiting the stage, show them to actors and crews and establish safety procedures.

   ■ Determine safe routes to use during blackouts or set changes to avoid hazards.

   ■ Use glow tape where necessary to mark changes in elevation (such as steps, stairs, or edges of platforms).

   ■ When not in use, barricade hazards such as open pits or traps and use glow tape on the edges.

6. Check the costume and makeup rooms for temperature and ventilation. If the space is tight and there is no window, a door can be blocked open with a window fan facing the hall. This will pull the stale air from the room without blowing things around (like powder or hair spray into an actor's eyes).

   A star performer refused to come out of the dressing room because of management cutting corners which the actors perceived as threatening to their health. I made recommendations to cancel a needed rehearsal in order to deal with the problems. The attention to their concerns made a difference in the actors' attitudes and a difference in the quality of the remaining rehearsals.

   —ERIC FORSYTHE, UNIVERSITY OF IOWA

7. Remind actors to avoid sharing makeup or reusable supplies such as sponges because of the danger of communicable diseases. Use spray pumps rather than aerosol. If latex or spirit gum is used, ventilate the space. Post a list of health and safety rules in the makeup rooms.

8. Set up spotting lights which will help actors find their way backstage during a blackout.

9. Be sure that food used on stage is prepared, handled, and preserved under safe and sanitary conditions.

10. After each technical rehearsal and performance, check all weapons and props which are potential hazards (like a rickety chair) and list those items which need adjustment or repair. A *repair sheet* should also be posted for actors and crew to note broken or damaged items.

11. If you are located in a control booth away from the backstage area during performances, assign a crew person (preferably an ASM), who has first-aid training, to respond to injuries and to report them to you.

12. Secure the facility.

PERFORMANCES

1. Post all warnings in the lobby concerning excessive fog effects, smoke, and so on. People who are allergic to or bothered by fog may choose to sit at the back or in higher seats to escape breathing it in.

   I sat through a black box performance of Macbeth *with the audience and actors immersed in fog for the entire play. I am not allergic, but I was annoyed. Some people chose to leave.*

   —DORIS SCHNEIDER

2. Most deaths in fires are due to smoke inhalation and panic. Plan and post the procedures for evacuating the theatre in case of an emergency. You should discuss this with the house manager since she/he will probably assist the audience while you assist the cast and crews. The procedure will vary with the theatre. If you have a fire curtain, assign a crew member the responsibility of cutting the line which releases the curtain. There may be a sprinkler system which comes on automatically. The following evacuation procedure should be evaluated for its effectiveness and adapted to suit your theatre and situation:

   - Announce on the P.A. system (in a calm voice) that the audience is to please leave the theatre immediately through the exit doors. Do not yell "Fire!" Through the backstage communications system, tell the ASMs to evacuate the cast and crew according to the prearranged plan with which everyone should be familiar.
   - Activate the fire alarm.
   - Call the fire department (as a back-up to the alarm) from a safe location.
   - Take a first-aid kit with you.
   - Shut doors behind you in order to contain smoke and fire.
   - Regroup at the planned location to determine if everyone is out and uninjured.
   - After everyone is accounted for, you can return to fight the fire with fire extinguishers—but only if it is safe to do so.

3. If actors are using live fire (such as lighted candles or oil lamps), they should have already discussed strategies for putting out a small accidental fire—in character.

   In an intimate scene in Desire Under the Elms, *two young actors accidentally knocked over an oil lamp. Instead of righting it and ad-libbing the moment, they chose to ignore it. The scene was lost because the*

*audience (waiting for the lamp and floor to burst into flames) couldn't
ignore it. Luckily the oil did not spill and the theatre still stands.*

—DORIS SCHNEIDER

However, had it burst into flames, *remember and remind your cast and
crews:* No one is expected to take risks. Costumes burn. Masks burn.
People burn.

4. Replace or reblock injured actors, dancers, or fighters. Do not allow a
    "the-show-must-go-on" attitude to worsen an already severe injury. You
    and the performer must honestly determine whether the injury is slight
    enough to allow the performer or the show to go on. Sometimes an un-
    scheduled intermission can give a performer time enough to get an ankle
    wrapped or to clear a spinning head. It also allows time to determine if the
    show can go on without the injured party. That is what understudies are
    for. In lieu of an understudy, move someone into the role who knows the
    show if not the lines. Unless it is the lead role, an audience can easily ac-
    cept someone carrying a book and reading lines. In fact, having witnessed
    the injury, they will usually applaud the effort.

5. After any injury during any phase of the production, fill out an *accident re-
    port* form as soon as possible.

> *NOTE: For additional strategies and concerns about stage combat and
> dance safety, read Chapters 5 and 6.*

STRIKE AND LOAD-OUT

1. Follow the same rules as load-in.
2. Remove all screws, nails, staples, and so on that can injure a crew person
    or other scenery or props.
3. Allow no unofficial, untrained helpers or gawkers. They may prove to be
    more hazard than help.

FIRST RESPONSE CARE

As stated earlier, this is not a first-aid course. Anyone truly interested in a career in stage management should become Red Cross certified and maintain
that certification by taking a refresher course every two years. The Red Cross
offers these courses at varied times to accommodate most schedules, and the
cost is small compared to the benefits. One of the OSHA rules is that there
should always be someone with first-aid training in the workplace. Identify

who is trained to give first aid so that you will know who to call on for assistance in an emergency.

GOOD SAMARITAN LAWS

Most states have Good Samaritan laws which give legal protection to people who provide emergency care to ill or injured persons. You can get information on your state's Good Samaritan laws at your local library or through a legal professional. These laws require that the "good Samaritan" use common sense and a reasonable level of skill, not to exceed the scope of his/her training. For example, you should:

1. Move a victim only if the victim's life is in danger.
2. Ask a conscious victim for permission before administering first aid.
3. Check the victim for life-threatening injuries to determine priority in giving care.
4. Call or send for professional help if the injuries are serious.
5. Continue to give care until professional help arrives.

Adherence to the above guidelines, in a reasonable and prudent manner, should protect you from liability. Always fill out an accident report (even for minor injuries), getting the signature of the victim or witnesses to validate the information.

DISEASE TRANSMISSION

In addition to protecting yourself from liability, you must also protect yourself and the victim from disease transmission, which can occur while giving care. Bacteria and viruses pass from one person to another by touching and breathing. Some diseases (such as tuberculosis) can be inhaled or injested while others (such as HIV) are passed through body fluids. You can help reduce chances of infection by following these guidelines:

1. Avoid contact with body fluids (especially blood, semen, or vaginal discharge).
2. Use disposable gloves or some other barrier between the victim's body fluids and yourself.
3. Cover any cuts, scrapes, or skin conditions you may have in order to protect the victim as well as yourself.
4. Immediately after giving care, wash your hands and any other skin which might have been contaminated. Do not eat, drink, or touch your mouth, nose, or eyes until this has been done.

FIRST-AID KITS

First-aid kits can be purchased at your local pharmacy or Red Cross chapter. If you make your own, stock only those things that you are likely to need and include (at least) the following:

1. Antiseptic ointment
2. Gauze pads and roller gauze (assorted sizes)
3. Adhesive tape
4. Scissors and tweezers
5. Disposable cold pack
6. Disposable gloves
7. Hand cleaner
8. Band-Aids (assorted sizes)
9. Elastic wraps (for sprains and strains)

If you are working at an outdoor theatre or on tour, you will need additional items such as:

10. Blanket
11. Snake-bite kit
12. Small flashlight with extra batteries
13. Triangular bandage

> NOTE: Your stage manager's kit (see Appendix A) should include all of the above so that you are prepared for emergency care-giving whether you are on stage, on a tour bus, or in a hotel room.

EMERGENCY CARE PROCEDURE

There are three steps to take in any emergency:

1. Check the scene to determine if it is a safe space to enter. (For example, if the victim is attached to live electricity, turn off the current or throw the master switch before giving aid or you, too, may become a victim.) If you cannot eliminate the danger, call your local emergency number immediately. Then wait for help.

2. Check the victim. If there is more than one victim, try to determine which is more seriously injured and give that person care first. Call your local emergency medical service (EMS) if any of the following conditions occur:

- The victim is or becomes unconscious
- The victim is not breathing or has difficulty breathing
- The victim has chest pain or pressure
- The victim has continuing pressure or pain in the abdomen
- The victim is vomiting or urinating blood
- The victim has a seizure, severe headache, or slurred speech
- The victim has injuries to the head, neck, or back
- The victim has possible broken bones
- The victim has burns covering more than one body part
- The victim has burns to the head, neck, hands, feet, or genitals
- The victim has burns from chemicals, explosions, or electricity
- The victim requests an ambulance
- You are in doubt about the seriousness of the injury

If the victim is conscious, ask what happened and what hurts. It may be easier to assess the seriousness of an injury if you know how it occurred. Witnesses can help. There is no definite rule about when an injury requires professional emergency care. You have to use your best judgement.

If possible, have someone else call so you can stay with the victim. Have the caller describe the injury and circumstances and stay on the phone until the dispatcher hangs up. The dispatcher may have important information concerning care you can give the victim while you wait for the ambulance. Send someone to the entrance of the theatre or building to guide the EMS personnel to the scene of the accident.

Do not move a seriously injured victim unless there is imminent danger such as fire, poisonous gas, falling objects, and so on.

Get permission from the victim to check for injuries and to administer first aid. In addition to the life-threatening conditions listed above, look for cuts, bruises, bumps, depressions, swelling, discoloration, and irregularity in body temperature. Look for a medical alert tag on the wrist or neck. It may provide important information on the victim's health or allergies to medications. The victim may be disoriented or have an injury to the mouth, limiting communication about pain and its sources.

3. Administer first aid.

ADDITIONAL DO'S AND DO NOT'S

This chapter does not teach CPR, rescue breathing, or other techniques that require hands-on experience with the equipment available in a first-aid class. The following is simply a common-sense list of recommendations:

1. Cover *open wounds* to control bleeding and prevent infection.

2. Use elastic bandages to control swelling and give support for injuries such as *sprains and strains*. Cold compresses and elevation also help to minimize swelling.

3. Do not remove an object (such as a knife) *impaled* in a *wound*. Wrap a dressing around the object to keep it in place until the victim can get advanced care.

4. Wrap a *severed body part* in sterile gauze and then place it in a plastic bag and put it on ice. Put it on the ambulance with the victim.

5. To control bleeding from a *knocked-out tooth,* place a sterile dressing in the gap and have the victim bite down on it.

6. Have a *nosebleed* victim lean forward and pinch the nostrils together.

7. Do not use home remedies on *burns*. Stop the burning; cool the skin with water (not ice); use a mild antibiotic on minor burns; and cover the burn with a loose dressing. Do not try to clean a severe burn or remove pieces of cloth that stick to the burn. Do not break blisters.

8. Do not cool an *electrical burn*. Cover it with a dry sterile dressing.

9. Treatment for *head and spine injuries* includes minimal movement of the head and spine, monitored consciousness and breathing, control of any external bleeding, and a regulation of temperature to avoid overheating or chilling.

10. Collect information on treatment from those cast and crew members that have medical problems that may require emergency procedures. *Diabetes, epilepsy, and severe asthma* are examples of common problems that can become life-threatening and require specialized medication or treatment. Designate a place for the medication to be kept during rehearsals and performances so you can find it if the victim is unconscious or unable to communicate.

In summary, *preparation, communication, organization,* and *anticipation* are still your greatest stage management tools even in guarding the health and safety of your company and audience.

8

STAGE MANAGEMENT AS A CAREER CHOICE

There is a need for experienced, competent stage managers in every branch of the entertainment industry: the stage, film, television, theme parks, concerts, or any presentation that requires coordination, communication, and cueing for performers and/or technical support. Each of these branches has its own unions, job descriptions, and employment procedures.

Career opportunities for stage managing live theatre (the focus of this book) are usually divided between New York theatres, regional theatres, community theatres, summer stock, outdoor dramas, and higher education. The jobs can vary from a few weeks of employment to a year-round salaried position. Most stage managers freelance and must move from one company or one production to another. Freelancing in any area of theatre is, at best, difficult and unstable. However, for some, this freedom of movement and choice is an appealing aspect of the job.

WHERE THE JOBS ARE LOCATED

New York productions range from short-running off-off-Broadway productions to long-running Broadway shows, which may be followed by a tour of the country and even abroad. The stage manager that originates a successful Broadway show may stay with it for years. Because of the enormous expense of these productions (especially musicals), only well-known and trusted individuals are contracted for the focal positions of production stage manager or stage manager. For this reason, many professionals say that if you want to stage manage in New York, the sooner you go there, join Equity, begin making contacts and developing a reputation, the better, but you should never by-pass an education. It will ultimately help you get where you are going faster and with more confidence.

Regional theatres are providing many opportunities for quality experience and improved job stability. Instead of being hired for one production, the PSM or SM may be contracted for a full-time staff position. This also usually requires Equity membership.

Non-Equity stage management jobs in community theatres can range from strictly volunteer work to well paid one-production or one-season assignments. Rarely do they offer a permanent year-round position.

Summer stock and outdoor dramas have a short season and provide opportunities for work experience while you are in school. Summer stock usually involves an intense work schedule and the mounting of multiple shows in an impossible amount of time. Everyone should do it at least once to test their own stamina and sharpen their troubleshooting skills. Outdoor dramas usually involve large casts representing a wide range of age and experience. It is a difficult assignment with a unique set of challenges created by the large cast, the weather, a heavy use of firearms and explosives, and an audience of tourists. The difficulties of working in these theatres can also be the advantages. Both often allow drama students more responsibilities and different experiences than they can get as undergraduates in an educational environment.

Stage managing in higher education is a growing job market. Many universities are hiring professional stage managers to teach one or more courses in stage management and to supervise the student stage managers for their season of shows. If it is a full-time teaching position, an advanced degree (MA or MFA) is usually required. Otherwise, it may be a temporary position without benefits (health insurance and retirement).

Alternative stage managing opportunities abound and are available as "good-experience-but-low-paying" summer jobs for students, spanning the continuum to high-paying professional-level employment. Alternative opportunities include theme parks such as Disney World or Busch Gardens, special events such as grand openings or parades, musical concerts that are heavy on special lighting and other effects, various levels of film-making from documentaries to motion pictures, and, of course, television.

Tracy Francis, AEA stage manager, is currently the production manager for *American Gladiators* (televised competition performed before a live audience in Orlando, Florida). He also stage manages special events such as an annual parade in Seoul, Korea.

Erica Neubert stage manages for a Renaissance Faire, a relatively new form of theme park. It is an interactive reenactment of Elizabethan life and times and has multiple outdoor stages which house different plays at regular intervals. There are more than fifty Renaissance Faires in the United States, so many stage management personnel are needed.

The Pennsylvania Renaissance Faire covers thirty acres of theatre. There are nine separate stage areas, with shows overlapping and running

Production stage manager Erica Neubert poses on a medieval wagon at the Pennsylvania Renaissance Faire. The PSM and other stage managers dress in costume for the Faire but wear a headset for communication. (Photo by Nancy Yoder)

simultaneously. The company is made up of 40–50 semiprofessionals (high school and college students and those having other careers), 15–20 professionals (those making a living as actors), and 40 independents (musical groups, jousters, etc. that job in). Thus you are overseeing a fluctuating cast of up to 110 people. All of this is run by one PSM (Erica Neubert), one full-time stage manager and one part-time stage manager. The gates open at 10:00 A.M. and don't close until the sun goes down. Anything can happen.

— DIANE CREWS, FREELANCE DIRECTOR, PLAYWRIGHT, AND EDUCATOR

CAREER LONGEVITY

Although some individuals elect stage management as a lifelong career, many find the hardships and insecurity of freelancing in a relatively stressful job are just too demanding. Most theatre artists must freelance but acting, directing, designing, and technical jobs do not carry the same burden of responsibility and commitment of time as does stage managing. However, the level of stress in a job is not as significant as the individual's ability to deal with stress.

As technology develops, productions become increasingly more complex, and therefore more dependent on organization. Everyone relies so heavily on the stage manager—the pressure during technical and dress rehearsals becomes inhuman, and the stage manager is very vulnerable. It is an unreasonable job, and I think the role should be reexamined.

—MING CHO LEE, SCENIC DESIGNER, YALE SCHOOL OF DRAMA

Not every stage-management position has the amount of responsibility and stress that Ming Cho Lee refers to in the above quote, and not everyone would agree with his point of view. However, it is important, especially for educators, to consider this viewpoint and reevaluate the position rather than continue to pile new responsibilities onto an already full plate.

Many people who begin as stage managers become discontented and make lateral moves to more stable positions in theatre management or move to jobs with more creative input, such as directing. Others stage manage just to be employed and change roles as soon as possible. Still others use stage management as a springboard, or more accurately, a rung in the ladder to their real goal. They may move from SM, to PSM, to assistant director, to director. That is similar to a publicist hoping to one day be a playwright. They are both in the same trade, using the same raw materials, and are interdependent, but the skills, artistry, and personality traits specific to each role are not necessarily interchangeable. That is not to say that a stage manager could not be a good director or that a director could not be a good stage manager. It is simply an indirect route. If you know that you want to be a director, experience as a stage manager will be very helpful; but years spent building a career as a

Barry Kornhauser, stage manager and playwright-in-residence, sits on the balcony of the Fulton Opera House. He has held a year-round staff position at the Fulton Opera House for fifteen years. (Photo by Marschka)

stage manager will be years taken away from preparation for directing. There is also the concern that you will be labeled a stage manager and not taken seriously as a director. On the other hand, years spent observing and working closely with directors can be equivalent to an exceptional internship.

I truly love what I do, but as I get older and want to move less, I'll probably want to move up into another creative aspect of production which is more stable.

—EVELYN MATTEN, AEA STAGE MANAGER

TRAINING OPTIONS

UNIVERSITY

Most drama students begin college with the ambition to become a star. Some begin in a completely different area of study, audition for a show, and are hooked for life—or until they find out how difficult a life it can be. Once hooked, they often find that their talents and interests are not necessarily on stage. It is important to have this time of discovery, to try on different hats, and to find the one that fits. The more you learn about theatre in general, the better theatre practitioner you will be—regardless of the role you ultimately choose to play.

Many universities do not have a formal course in stage management, although the number that do is growing each year. The purpose of the course is often just to prepare students to stage manage the department productions and consequently there is very little lecture and lots of practicum. This is not bad, but it also is not ideal. If you are shopping for a university to attend, make sure they have at least one stage management course and an experienced stage manager teaching it.

If you are already in a drama program that does not offer stage management courses or training, you can remedy the problem by working with professional or at least very experienced stage managers in other theatres during the summer. A stock company, an outdoor drama, or a professional company connected to your university can provide work or internship opportunities. Do not be surprised if your first summer job requires you to do menial tasks. Do them well, volunteer to help on projects that give you more knowledge, learn through observation, and make contacts. For the second summer job, you may return to the same company where you are a known quantity and apply for a stage-management position with more responsibility.

UNDERGRADUATE PROFESSIONAL SCHOOLS

Professional schools generally stress early specialization and are suited only to those students who are very focused on specific career goals. Bachelor of

Fine Arts (BFA) programs that consider their degrees to be final preparation for the professional theatre fit into this category. There is much controversy about whether this type of education is adequate for all theatre artists. However, some BFA programs have a broad liberal arts and theatre arts curriculum in addition to advanced courses for the purpose of specialization.

The positive aspect of early specialization is that you will have a very direct route to stage-management jobs in professional theatres following graduation. The negative side is that you may not have had time to gain the general knowledge and maturity necessary to do the job well. If you decide later that you want to develop some other career in theatre or in another field, you will have to begin from scratch. If you choose a professional school which focuses strictly on your area of interest, supplement your education by electing courses that will broaden your knowledge and look for opportunities to gain additional types of theatre experience.

GRADUATE SCHOOLS

Many universities with graduate studies in theatre are developing Master of Fine Arts (MFA) programs in stage management. They are often tied to another area of study such as directing, management, or technical theatre. Knowledge in each of these areas would be of great value to any stage manager. Choose a program that allows you to combine stage management with the area that you foresee as a possible alternative career choice. This would also give you an additional subject area should you decide to teach. The added plus of a master's degree is that it makes you eligible to apply for that teaching position in higher education.

> *Whatever training you can get in every aspect of technical theatre – do it. It will give you a language as well as allow you to anticipate, understand, and communicate to the shops what is needed to support the action of the show.*
>
> —CRAIG WEINDLING, AEA STAGE MANAGER

Stage managers who attend graduate school usually fit into one of the following categories: They come from undergraduate programs which have not prepared them for this career; they chose their area of specialization late in their undergraduate studies and need the information and contacts they can get in graduate school; they are academically oriented and want to pursue another degree while they have the opportunity and want the option of teaching in higher education at some later time; or they have been working as stage managers and simply feel a need for updating and augmenting their theatre knowledge. If you are going back to school, why get more undergraduate credits if you can work towards a graduate degree instead?

Beware of the graduate program that offers you very little opportunity to learn other than by stage managing all of their productions. They may be just getting free labor. Interview other graduate students in the program you are considering. They can give you feedback on the value of their program.

APPRENTICESHIPS AND INTERNSHIPS

An alternative to graduate school is an apprenticeship training program. Apprenticeships are often unpaid positions, or they may pay only enough for room and board. Another term which is sometimes used interchangeably with apprenticeship is "internship." Internships are usually salaried positions. As an apprentice, you are learning your craft; as an intern, you are practicing it under supervision. If you are not confident about your skills as a stage manager, these are good choices and are available in some excellent professional companies such as Arena Stage (Washington, D.C.) and Crossroads (New Jersey). They also provide you the chance to prove yourself in a respected theatre environment, which will enrich your resumé and allow you to make good future job contacts.

MENTOR SYSTEM

Another alternative to graduate and/or undergraduate training is to learn the art and craft through a mentor stage manager. A professional stage manager may be willing to take a promising hardworking individual as an assistant and teach in a one-on-one situation. Choose a mentor with a wide range of experience whose recommendations and contacts will help you find work later.

WORKING YOUR WAY UP

If you want to bypass college or already have a degree in something else but want a career in stage management, it can be done. Work (for pay or not for pay) at the best theatre available to you. Apply for a position as a production assistant. Any crew work will be good experience for you and will add to your resumé. Make yourself known and valuable through your enthusiasm and hard work. Your next step is to assistant stage manager, then to stage manager. If possible, take course work to increase your general theatre knowledge and take the initiative to read and learn on your own.

Stage managers are hired most often through personal contacts and recommendations from other professionals. College and graduate degrees can be important for gaining the knowledge, experience, and maturity to carry out the tasks, but they will not guarantee you continued employment. Each opportunity you have to work on any aspect of a production will give you more preparation for stage management, and each person you work with is a potential contact and a possible future employer.

A recently deceased and dearly loved stage manager in New York once said, "If they want to stage manage, tell them to leave home, come to New York, and start learning the trade." He had dropped out of university and done that very thing many years before and was quite successful. However, he also said that he felt very insecure about his lack of technical knowledge and knew that he would have benefitted from more education. The problem was that there was no training for stage management in higher education at that time. Well, the times they are a changin'!

PROFESSIONAL ASSOCIATIONS

ACTORS' EQUITY ASSOCIATION (AEA)

AEA is the union for stage actors and stage managers. Getting membership was described at the beginning of this text as a catch-22 experience. You cannot get union membership without a professional contract; you cannot get a contract without union membership. There is a way around it. Through the Membership Candidate Program, you can earn membership by earning points for weeks worked in a company that is authorized to offer the program. Alternatively, a professional company can offer you a contract, making you eligible for membership. You must complete a registration form and pay a registration fee. There are also annual membership dues and an initiation fee.

Membership in AEA provides many privileges and benefits. Equity negotiates minimum wages and working conditions, generally requiring a bond covering at least two weeks salary and pension and health insurance payments for each member of a production.

If you are serious about a career in stage management, you will ultimately want membership in AEA. However, do not be in a rush to get your Equity card. Once you have it, you will not be allowed to legally work non-Equity (without minimum wage, benefits, etc.). Get the knowledge, experience, and resumé necessary to assure producers that you are a capable stage manager before limiting yourself to union contracts which may be few and far between. Before joining the union, get to know it through reading the handbook and by talking to other Equity members.

For information and a copy of the AEA Handbook, write or call:

Actors' Equity Association
National Office
165 West 46th Street
New York, NY 10036
(212) 869–8530

AMERICAN GUILD FOR MUSICAL ARTISTS (AGMA)

The American Guild of Musical Artists represents dancers, concert and operatic singers (including both soloists and choristers), as well as stage directors, stage managers, narrators, and other performers in the fields of music, concert, recital, dance, oratorio, and opera.

The Guild's mission is to advance, foster, promote, and benefit all those concerned with the fields listed above; to eliminate unfair practices and abuses in these professions; to promote the mutual aims and interests of artists; and to enhance musical arts and culture in this country.

For information, write or call:

American Guild of Musical Artists
1727 Broadway
New York, NY 10019-5284
(212) 265–3687

For information on membership to AGMA, contact the supervisor of membership at the above address.

STAGE MANAGERS' ASSOCIATION (SMA)

This is an international organization of professional stage managers. Eight meetings are held each year in New York. Transcripts of these meetings and forums between stage managers and various professionals from diverse theatre disciplines, as well as current contact sheets are sent to the full membership. The SMA publishes the annual *Stage Managers' Directory*, which includes resumés of stage managers and can be used by producers to select and contact personnel for new shows. SMA also has a program called "Operation Observation" through which members can observe other stage managers working their shows—a significant opportunity for learning.

For information, write or call:

The Stage Managers' Association
P.O. Box 2234, Times Square Station
New York, NY 10108-2020
(212) 691–5633

UNITED STATES INSTITUTE FOR THEATRE TECHNOLOGY (USITT)

This organization was established primarily for design and production professionals in the performing arts. It sponsors regional meetings throughout the year as well as an annual national conference which includes workshops, masters' classes, and informational meetings on various aspects of technical theatre. Stage management is one of their major divisions of interest. They publish a quarterly journal called *Theatre Design and Technology* (TD&T) and a newsletter, *Sightlines*. USITT publishes additional literature related to the profession such as *Theatre Words*, a multilanguage glossary of technical theatre terms, and an annual *Internship Directory*, providing listings of more than 1,000 internships in stage management, design, technical production, and so on. USITT is the United States Center of OISTAT, Organisation Internationale des Scénographes, Techniciens et Architectes de Théâtre.

For information, write or call:

USITT
10 West 19th Street, Suite 5A
New York, NY 10011-4206
(212) 924-9088

STATE AND REGIONAL THEATRE CONFERENCES

State and regional theatre conferences are held each fall and spring respectively. In addition to workshops and presentations on various aspects of the theatre, they host auditions and interviews for summer jobs. For addresses and phone numbers of your state and regional organizations, call a university drama department in your area.

AMERICAN THEATRE IN HIGHER EDUCATION

The national organization for educational theatre meets annually in August and provides workshops and presentations directed to the university educator. They also have a job placement division to which you can subscribe and send resumés. This is primarily for positions in colleges and universities and resident theatres associated with an educational institution.

American Theatre in Higher Education
THEatre SERVICE
P.O. Box 15282
Evansville, IN 47716-0282

THEATRE DIRECTORIES

There are several directories which list regional and summer theatres offering internships, apprenticeships, and staff positions. They specify the number of vacant positions and criteria for application.

Summer Theatre Directories
P.O. Box 519
Dorset, VT 05251
(802) 867-2223

Regional Theatre Directories
P.O. Box 519
Dorset, VT 05251
(802) 867-2223

USITT Internship Directory
10 W. 19th Street, Suite 5A
New York, NY 10011-4206
(212) 924-9088

There are also two directories which list and describe undergraduate and graduate programs in theatre.

Directory of Theatre Training Programs
P.O. Box 519
Dorset, VT 05251
(802) 867–2223

Directory of the Graduate Theatre Training Programs
University/Resident Theatre Association
1560 Broadway, Room 903
New York, NY 10036
(212) 221–1130

PUBLICATIONS AND ORGANIZATIONS WITH JOB LISTINGS

Several publications include job listings and are especially beneficial to the freelancing professional theatre practitioner. Some are specifically for theatre jobs in New York City. For example, The Alliance of Resident Theatres/New York (ART/New York) maintains the *Job Book,* a listing of employment opportunities in New York theatres, and the *Resume Book,* which includes resumés of stage managers and other technical personnel.

The Alliance of Resident Theatres/New York
131 Varick Street, Room 904
New York, NY 10019
(212) 586–6343

The *Theatrical Index* lists job information for every theatre in New York, both currently running and in the planning.

Theatrical Index
888 Eighth Avenue
New York, NY 10019
(212) 586–6343

Artsearch, the National Employment Service Bulletin for the Arts, is published by Theatre Communications Group (TCG).

Artsearch
c/o TCG
355 Lexington Avenue
New York, NY 10017

RESUMÉS, PORTFOLIOS, AND INTERVIEWS

The results of a national survey conducted by the author and her colleague, Johnny Alston, lead to the development of the following criteria for resumés,

letters of introduction, portfolios, and interviews. The survey included responses from educational, professional, and summer theatres. The most commonly requested ingredients for the above included *specific information,*
brevity, and *honesty.*

RESUMÉS

1. *Length:* Resumés vary in length and content according to the applicant's
   goal. If you are seeking acceptance into a graduate program, you will include all theatre experience and education (formal and informal). This
   may take several pages, but educators are interested in the breadth of your
   theatre knowledge as well as your stage management experience. Official
   undergraduate grade transcripts will accompany the resumé as well as a
   cover letter stating your degree plans and career objectives.

   If you are applying for a teaching position, you will include all of the
   above as well as any teaching credentials and National Teacher Exam
   (NTE) test results. There is currently a teacher shortage in the arts in
   many states, providing the opportunity to teach while completing teacher
   certification requirements.

   If you are seeking employment as a professional stage manager, reduce
   your resumé to one page and provide only that experience which speaks
   of your ability to stage manage. If your application is being mailed prior to
   an interview, include a letter of introduction. If you have more experience
   than you can get on one page, keep recent listings and those which demonstrate your range and flexibility; group or summarize the rest.

2. *Content:* Specific content for all stage manager resumés includes the
   following:

   - Name
   - Complete contact information (permanent and nonpermanent)
   - Photo*
   - Union affiliations (if any)
   - Theatre experience (including titles of shows, assigned roles, produc-
     tion dates, production companies, and locations)
   - Related theatre experience (especially technical and management)
   - Related skills (first-aid training, computer literacy, accounting, etc.)
   - Training/education
   - Age (optional)
   - Three references

---

*The photo may be printed on the resumé or attached. Its main purpose is to help the
interviewer recall the interviewee.

3. *Format:* There are many acceptable formats for organizing the information in a resumé and for presenting a pleasing appearance. The major considerations are a readable type size and style, headings and subheadings that can be easily seen (in the margin or in bold or larger type), and a logical order of information. Many desktop publishing companies or quick-copy printers keep samples of resumés from which you can choose an appealing format. Keep your resumé on a computer disk so it can be regularly updated.

4. *References:* Most interviewers expect three references. Provide names, addresses, phone numbers, and fax numbers. Written recommendations are usually not necessary unless they are requested. Many companies or universities have their own recommendation form which they send out to assure confidentiality.

LETTERS OF INTRODUCTION

Whenever a resume is mailed to a potential employer or graduate program, it should be accompanied by a one-page letter of introduction (cover letter).

1. *Content:*

   - *Paragraph 1:* Get attention! State the purpose of your letter.

   - *Paragraph 2:* Arouse interest! Establish an understanding and support of the interviewing organization's mission/philosophy. Refer to the opening or need that you can fill and relate this opportunity to your stated career goals.

   - *Paragraph 3:* Sell Yourself! Summarize education and experience that make you a desirable candidate for the position and mention specific skills that give you a competitive edge. Refer to the accompanying resumé for more details.

   - *Paragraph 4:* Request action! Ask for application forms, ask for an interview, or ask for the job. Give your dates of availability both to interview and to begin work.

2. *Suggestions:*

   - Personalize the letter to the interviewer and organization. Do not write "To whom it may concern" or "Dear Sir." It is worth the time and cost of a phone call to get the correct name and title of the interviewer.

   - Keep the letter short, natural, and concise.

   - Type the letter and proofread it.

   - Make a copy for your file.

   - Do not request a phone call to set up an interview. Follow the letter with your own phone call to set a time and place. Persistence indicates real interest and confidence, but do not be a pest or pushy.

LETTERS OF RECOMMENDATION

It is usually not necessary to send letters of recommendation with the resumé and letter of introduction. However, it is wise to collect letters of recommendation from teachers, directors, producers, or crew supervisors with whom you have had a good production experience while this experience is still fresh in their minds. Include the letters in your portfolio and make them available at the interview.

1. *Content:* Regardless of the position you held under the recommender's supervision, you may ask him/her to refer to those qualities that suggest your potential for success as a stage manager:

   - Personal discipline
   - Professional integrity
   - Organizational, leadership, and people skills

2. *Suggestions:* You can note on your resumé that letters of recommendation are available on request.
   - Include letters that refer to the skills related to the position for which you are applying.
   - Include current rather than old letters.
   - Include letters from persons who are more likely to be recognized by and command the respect of the interviewer.

PORTFOLIO

Although a stage manager's portfolio is less important than a good interview and positive recommendations, it nevertheless should not be overlooked.

1. *Content:* Your portfolio should include a copy of your resumé, letters of recommendation, production books, and production photographs. If you are applying for graduate school acceptance, the content should also include representations of any technical, management, or directing experience from production or classroom projects.

   - Even if you mailed a resumé in advance, have one in your portfolio and an additional copy for each interviewer.
   - Include two or three letters of recommendation that speak very well of you. Additional letters that are lukewarm or hesitant in their support of your work will hurt rather than help you.
   - Select two or three production books that demonstrate your organizational skills, your attention to clarity and detail, and your thoroughness. Take the time to clean up a messy or incomplete book before using it to represent your work. Refer to Chapter 4 for information on

production book content. If you used two books for a production (one for rehearsals and one to call cues), include both. Also include in the book one or two photographs of the show.

■ Include a few photographs of other productions to reflect the quality and variety of shows you have stage managed. Label photographs with production title, theatre, and dates.

2. *Organization:* Keep all materials except the production books in a notebook or presentational portfolio case. Arrange the entries in a logical order for discussion during an interview. If possible, purchase or build a carrying case which houses all of your presentational materials. You may have to carry the portfolio and books a long distance between your transportation and the interview office.

3. *Recommendations:* Begin collecting materials for your portfolio now. Keep everything. You may never use some of it but it will give content choices until you have enough experience to edit out all extraneous information. Even programs can be important to verify your role in a production as well as providing other information and names which might be useful for future job contacts.

■ Stay flexible. Choose resumé and portfolio content to suit the position for which you are applying. Keep other materials organized and filed for future use.

■ Do not use materials for which you must make excuses. If you have limited experience, choose production books which best represent your capabilities and be prepared to discuss in a positive light any weaknesses in these books.

■ If you have varied experience, select books which demonstrate your range and your ability to complement the production or the company mission. For example, if you are interviewing for a company that produces new experimental scripts on a shoestring budget, choose a production book that conveys your ability to work with nonconventional concepts and that emphasizes economy and efficiency in scheduling rehearsals and work crews.

■ Use *no* photographs rather than *poor* photographs. Some quick-copy print shops can make enlarged good quality copies of photographs from negatives, slides, or prints at a reasonable price.

■ *Be honest in the content of your portfolio of work.* It is difficult, if not impossible, to rebuild trust after destroying it.

PORTFOLIO PRESENTATION AND INTERVIEW

An interview for a stage manager is often more casual than formal because of the need to assess the applicant's personality and people skills. However, preliminary planning as well as follow-up can make a big difference in the success of an interview.

1. *Preliminary Planning:* Get as much information about the interview as possible from your primary contact (prospective employer, program chair, office manager, etc.).

   - Verify the time for the interview and get directions to the location. If you are driving, get parking information.
   - If it has not been made clear already, get a complete job description. Whether it is full-time employment or an assistantship in a graduate program, you need to know which skills and knowledge your portfolio should reflect in order to organize it and prepare your oral presentation.
   - Ask about the number of interviewers and their names and areas of specialization.
   - Ask about the time allocated for the interview.
   - Ask about other opportunities for you to assess the program or company. You may request to tour the facility and to meet other students, staff, or employees. Besides giving you information, this demonstrates your interest in the theatre and company.
   - Make a list of your own questions.
   - Dress appropriately.
   - Bring pen, paper, and calendar for noting information and dates during and after the interview.
   - *Be prompt.*

2. *Interview:* In interviewing for a stage-management position or acceptance into a graduate program, you should be prepared with a practiced oral presentation of your portfolio and a readiness to answer questions about your production books and other documentation. Additional suggestions include the following:

   - Do not chew gum.
   - Do not smoke unless others are smoking and it is offered.
   - Be relaxed and natural, sincere and enthusiastic, friendly and polite.
   - Be prepared to discuss production problems and problem-solving techniques, particularly those related to people management and stress management. Do not refer to particular individuals but to situations.
   - Be positive about previous theatre experiences and personalities. Do not speak negatively of other companies or colleagues.
   - Demonstrate a familiarity with the interviewing company's mission/philosophy.

- Ask your own questions about the company, policies, and so on.

- Show commitment to the art of theatre and show respect for and an understanding of the contributions of the entire production staff and crews.

- Show tolerance, confidence, honesty, and a *sense of humor.*

3. *Portfolio Presentation:* Use your best communication skills while demonstrating your organization skills through a well-prepared oral presentation of portfolio materials that are arranged in a logical sequence.

   - The presentation of your portfolio materials may be naturally integrated into the interview or you may be given a set amount of time for that purpose. Allow the interviewer(s) to control the flow of the meeting unless there is a time limit and too much time has been spent on one part of the portfolio, preventing you from completing your presentation. Tactfully turn the discussion to other areas.

   - Provide an opportunity for questions about your portfolio content.

   - Do not be defensive or argumentative about criticism. Above all, do not blame someone else for weaknesses in your portfolio content or your contributions to a production. Rather, tell how you would solve the problem should it reoccur.

4. *Conclusion and Follow-up:* Be prepared to summarize your skills, experience, and the unique qualities that make you the right person for the job or graduate program. Thank the interviewer(s).

Follow up the interview with a thank-you note. After an appropriate time has passed, make a phone call to inquire politely about the status of your application and the results of your interview. Persistence in pursuing a goal often pays off and indicates determination and interest.

EPILOGUE

The theatre as an art form continues to evolve both intellectually and technologically. Therefore, on every level you must assume the attitude that wherever you are in your career, you will continue to learn in order to participate in the development of new visions. As a collaborator, you must listen not only with an open heart and mind for the voice of a colleague's muse, you must also evoke the gentle voice of your own.

STAGE MANAGER'S KIT

A

Edit the following list to meet the needs of your cast and crew.

- First-aid instruction booklet
- Sterile gloves
- Ice packs
- Elastic bandages (for wrapping ankles, knees, or elbows)
- Smelling salts
- Antiseptic wipes
- Hydrogen peroxide
- Antiseptic cream or spray
- Burn cream or spray
- Needle and tweezers (for splinters)
- Bandages, sterile pads, gauze, surgical tape
- Eye wash and eye pads
- Pain medicine (aspirin, nonaspirin, other)
- Throat lozenges
- Antacid tablets (and other digestion medication)
- Soap
- Tissues
- Feminine hygiene products
- Mouthwash or breath spray
- Hairpins and tiebacks
- Safety pins, straight pins, sewing needles, and thread

A stage manager's kit bag needs several pouches to properly organize its contents. An inexpensive travel bag or gym bag, with handles, is easy to carry and very suitable when the production goes on the road. (Photo by J. B. Alston)

- Scissors
- Tailor's measuring tape
- Stopwatch
- Adhesive-backed note paper
- Matches
- Transparent tape
- Masking tape (1″ and 1/2″)
- No. 2 pencils
- Erasers
- Pencil sharpener
- Whistle
- Flashlight
- Luminous tape
- Electrical tape
- Tacks or pushpins
- Stapler and staples
- Paper clips

- Hole punch
- Extra batteries in protective packaging
- Magic markers
- Scale rule
- Measuring tape (25'–30')
- Chalk

TECHNICAL LETTERING   B

Lettering is freehand drawing, not writing. Good lettering is accomplished by conscious effort. The ability to letter has little relationship to the ability to write. Excellent letterers often have poor handwriting. The following instructions are not as rigid as those required for achieving draftsman-quality lettering. They are brief and basic and will enable you to produce legible lettering for memos, forms, signs, blocking notes, and so on.

> *Although lettering exercises may seem like an elementary school project, a few minutes spent on these pages can improve your legibility significantly. When I expressed concern about including this appendix because some readers found it too basic, my students unanimously said, "NO!" They claimed that this skill (having practiced it one time) has greatly influenced their ability to hand-letter and made a real difference.*
>
> —DORIS SCHNEIDER

UNIFORMITY

The key to good lettering is uniformity in

1. Height
2. Proportion
3. Inclination (slant)
4. Boldness of line
5. Spacing of letters
6. Spacing of words

Lightly drawn horizontal guidelines are essential early on for maintaining consistency in height. These lines can be drawn with a pencil and straight edge. However, the more lettering you do, the better you will become at measuring with your eyes to maintain a consistency sufficient for the tasks required of a stage manager.

A good visual image of the letter is necessary for accurate reproduction of its proportions. That means you have to look analytically at each letter on the worksheet and note *where* horizontal and inclined or curved strokes meet vertical lines.

Example: The second stroke of the letter K meets the first stroke below its center, and the third stroke begins at the center of the second. The arrow indicates the direction of the stroke and the number indicates the order of the stroke.

TECHNIQUE

1. Horizontal strokes are drawn to the right.

2. Vertical, inclined, and curved strokes are drawn downward.

3. Use a pen or sharp pencil for uniformity of line width (boldness).

4. Space words well apart but space letters closely within words. Allow the space of the letter *O* between words.

The following are samples of letter spacing:

incorrect

WILL YOU

correct

WILL YOU

The following are samples of word spacing:

incorrect

NOFOOD ORDRINKS ALLOWED

correct

NO FOOD OR DRINKS ALLOWED

CREATIVITY

Only capital letters are recommended in order to maintain consistency through simplicity. However, that does not mean you must be boring. You can personalize your lettering by choosing a unique way to represent one or more letters or by beginning or ending words or statements in a unique way. Do not adopt any changes which will make your lettering less legible.

Samples:

GROUND PLAN

(Individualized letters are usually only used as an initial or final letter in a word.)

SCENERY STRIKE

(The words above were drawn on a straight edge, creating an even flat bottom line and maintaining consistency in style.)

REPORT

(Enlarged letters can be used to begin names or sentences as if you were using capital and lowercase letters.)

BLOCK LETTERING GUIDE

Study the printed letters with respect to proportion, order of strokes, and direction of strokes. Practice the letters in the space provided.

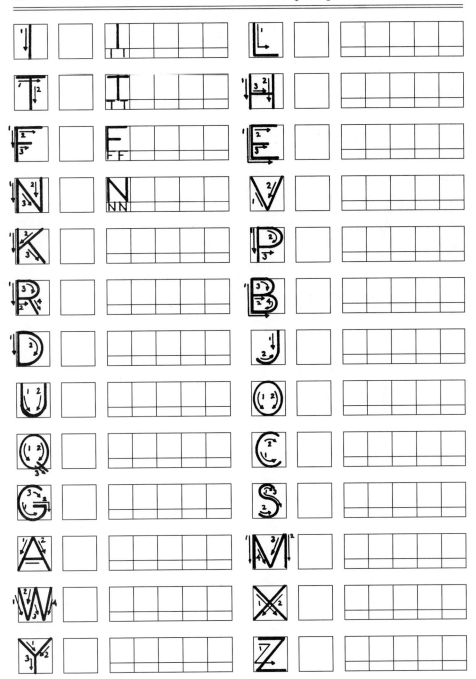

BLOCK NUMBERING GUIDE

Study the printed numbers with respect to proportion, order of strokes, and direction of strokes. Practice the numbers in the space provided.

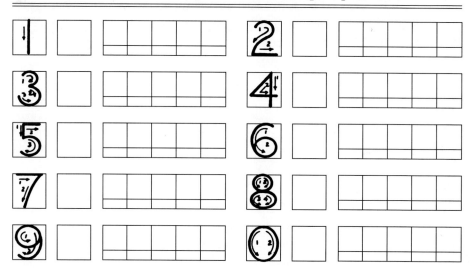

COMPANY RULES

By the end of the first rehearsal, each actor must complete and sign the signature sheet of the company rules to signify his/her understanding and acceptance of the content of the document.

DUTIES OF THE ACTOR

The actor agrees to the following:

To demonstrate respect for the production by maintaining the integrity of the playwright's script, the director's interpretation of the script, the designers' concepts for costumes and makeup, and by prompt attendance for all calls including (but not limited to) rehearsals, performances, costume fittings, and photo shoots;

To demonstrate respect for the production family through polite and ethical behavior and through prompt attendance for all calls;

To demonstrate respect for the physical property of the production and the theatre and to abide by all rules and regulations of the theatre and the production company including prompt attendance for all calls.

REHEARSALS

1. Actors must be ready to rehearse at the time called. If an actor is scheduled to rehearse at 7:00 P.M., he/she should plan to arrive no later than 6:50 P.M. in order to be ready by 7:00 P.M. Actors should *always* have their scripts and pencils (musical scores should never be marked in ink) and should wear appropriate rehearsal clothes.

Harcourt Brace & Company

2. If an actor is going to be late or cannot make a rehearsal, he/she must do the following:

   - call the stage manager, director, or the company office at least two hours before the rehearsal;
   - or leave a note on the callboard or in the director's mailbox as early as possible (if no one can be reached in person or by phone);
   - and have an acceptable reason for tardiness or absence.

3. If an actor has a conflict with rehearsal on a given day, it must be discussed with and approved by the director within the first week of rehearsals.

4. Upon arriving at rehearsal, actors must sign in with the stage manager. If an actor leaves the rehearsal facility, he/she must inform the stage manager.

5. Entrances and exits from the rehearsal space should be done only when there is a break or pause in the rehearsal.

6. No smoking, food, or drinks are allowed in the theatre. Under no circumstances will drugs or alcohol be tolerated before or during rehearsals or performances.

7. All calls, including rehearsals, will be posted on the callboard at least twenty-four hours in advance. However, if rehearsal circumstances demand it, a director may post the next day's call at the completion of the evening's rehearsal.

8. Changes in the rehearsal schedule will be posted on the callboard and announced at rehearsals. Check the callboard daily.

9. Canceled rehearsals due to inclement weather or other emergency situations will be communicated by phone and posted on the callboard. Actors must inform the stage manager of any changes in contact information.

10. Depending on the nature and needs of the production, actors may be called to rehearse or warm up prior to the performance. For example, participants in stage combat, singing, or dance may require an earlier call.

11. During rehearsals and performances, all directions and requests from the stage manager are to be acknowledged with a polite "thank you," confirming that the actor has heard and accepted the information.

12. Actors will maintain the integrity of the production by avoiding any changes in script, character interpretation, blocking, timing, costumes, and makeup once these have been set by the director and designers.

13. Actors will use the appropriate procedure for registering complaints rather than undermining the production with unethical behavior, gossip, or attitudes.

14. The director has the right to drop an actor, stage manager, or crew member from the production should their behavior become disruptive.

Harcourt Brace & Company

HEALTH AND SAFETY

1. The company accepts no responsibility if an actor is ill or injured. Actors are responsible for health and safety guidelines. Under no circumstances will pressure be placed on a person to perform if he/she feels unable. If ill or injured, the decision regarding coming to rehearsals or performing is the actor's.

2. No actors will be required to do anything that they feel is dangerous or unhealthy. If an actor feels that the task is dangerous, he/she must bring it to the attention of the stage manager or technical director. After consultation with the director or producer, a decision will be reached as to whether or not the task will be performed.

3. Actors and crews will report unsafe use of any hazardous materials, chemicals, or any unsafe actions in the rehearsal, performance, or work space to the director or stage manager.

4. Actors will refrain from any horseplay which might be viewed as dangerous.

PROGRAM AND BIOGRAPHICAL MATERIAL

1. Actors shall cooperate with the publicity office in the preparation of program, biographical, and other promotional materials and provide information as requested.

2. Actors shall have the right of approval of biographical material for the program and related materials prior to printing.

3. The program copy is to be posted on the callboard, with a deadline clearly stated for corrections and changes that will be made and initialed by each actor.

SECURITY

1. Actors are responsible for their own valuables. Neither the stage manager nor the production company is legally responsible for lost or stolen items. The SM will make provisions for holding valuables at the actor's request, but will not be legally responsible for them.

2. During rehearsals, no one is to be allowed backstage or in the dressing rooms except the actors, assigned crews, and theatre staff.

MAKEUP AND COSTUMES

1. Actors must provide all conventional makeup, not including nontraditional character makeup required by the costume designer or director.

2. Costume fittings will be scheduled during nonrehearsal hours. All fittings must be arranged through the stage manager. The stage manager will de-

termine the availability of the costumer and designer and coordinate this with the actor.

3. All makeup should be applied before costumes are put on.

4. Actors must wear their complete costumes during all dress rehearsals and performances, including the curtain call. No additions or deletions can be made to the design unless approved.

5. Actors must not eat, drink, or smoke in costume; they may not smoke at all in the dressing rooms.

6. It is the costumer's responsibility to place a complete costume in the actor's dressing room prior to the scheduled call. It is then the actor's responsibility to make sure the entire costume is returned to the dressing room after rehearsal or performance. A dresser may help an actor change and agree to return the costume to the dressing room, but it is ultimately the actor's responsibility to make sure that all parts of the costume are returned.

7. It is the actor's responsibility to hang up his/her costume in the dressing room after use. Heavy costumes should be turned inside-out to dry.

8. No part of the costume is allowed to be taken from the theatre without the designer's or costumer's approval, including parts of the costume belonging to the actor.

9. Actors must report in writing to the running crew any repairs, stains, or problems needing attention. A repair list will be placed by the costume crew in both the women's and men's dressing rooms for this purpose.

PROPS

1. Each actor is responsible for checking on his/her properties before each rehearsal and performance. All props carried off stage by actors should be returned to the prop table.

2. Props should not be handled except by the property person or by the actor using them. They are not to be played with, removed from the theatre, or used as tools, ashtrays, and so on. No one is to handle weapons except the assigned actor, stage manager, or fight captain.

3. Each actor is responsible for reporting on repair sheets any damaged prop. If the damaged prop creates a safety hazard, the actor should not use it again until it has been properly repaired.

ACTING DEPUTY

1. On the first day of rehearsals, a deputy will be elected by the cast members. The stage manager may conduct the election but is not elegible for election.

2. The deputy's duties include monitoring the adherence of the director and stage manager to company rules and policies. He/she will act as the cast

Harcourt Brace & Company

spokesperson if adjustments need to be made or a conflict arises regarding policies.

STRIKE

All members of the cast and crews are responsible for assisting with strike.* The date of strike is listed on the production calendar. Absolutely no props or costumes are to be considered the property of actors and all costumes and props must be accounted for. In some cases, especially musicals, personal notations on all scores must be erased and returned to the stage manager.

The following is an example of a company rules signature sheet:

After reading the company rules, sign below and return this page only to the stage manager. Your signature denotes understanding of and compliance with the stated rules.

I have read the company rules for the Department of Theatre at _____, I understand the information presented, and I agree to abide by the Department policies.

_____   _____
Name   Date

_____

*Full company strikes are not allowed by Equity, but they are often required by community and educational theatres, depending on the size of the crews and the philosophy of the staff.

Harcourt Brace & Company

Taping the ground plan means transferring a technical drawing to the stage or rehearsal floor so that the director can plan the movements of the actors, knowing the whereabouts of levels, vertical scenery, furniture, and entrances–all very important to blocking.

A **ground plan** is a diagram drawn to scale identifying the positions of all of the above and more. It is drawn like a map, as if you were above the stage looking down on the scenery.

Scale means the drawing is an exact duplicate of the space in a reduced size. The scale of reduction is usually 1/2″ = 1′-0″ or 1/4″ = 1′-0″. To determine which scale is used in your drawing, read the title block usually located in the lower right corner (see Figure D-1).

A *scale ruler,* sometimes called an architect's rule, is used to make the measurements and to read them. This ruler has three sides, and each side has four different scales, which can be used for measuring (see Figure D-2a). Figure D-2b represents the surface you will use most often. It includes these scales: one inch, one-half inch, one-fourth inch, and one-eighth inch.

Each scale is sectioned like any ruler except it is for reading feet rather than inches. Look at the one-half inch scale. The first section is subdivided to allow you to read inches and half-inches (see Figure D-3a). The remainder is divided for measuring feet. To measure the distance from point A to point B, place the ruler on zero at point B (see Figure D-3b). If point A falls between two sections of the ruler, move the ruler so that point A lines up with the lower of the two numbers it falls between. That number indicates feet and the inches are indicated by point B on the first section (see Figure D-3c).

Request a blueprint or photocopy of the ground plan and go over it with the scene designer to make sure you are interpreting the drawing accurately. Figure D-4 gives a few basic technical drawing conventions that will help you read the ground plan.

Students tape a ground plan to the stage floor under the direction of Rick Cunning-ham (center at table), head of stage management training at the University of Delaware. (Photo by Erik Alberg)

FIGURE D.1   TAPING THE GROUND PLAN

GROUND PLAN
BLUES IN THE NIGHT
NCCU DEPT. of DRAMATIC ART

PLATE NO.	DESIGNER: D. HELTON
1 OF 2	TECH. DIR.: J. ALSTON
	DRAWN BY: DH
SCALE: 1/2" = 1'-0"	DATE: 1-12-95

FIGURES D.2

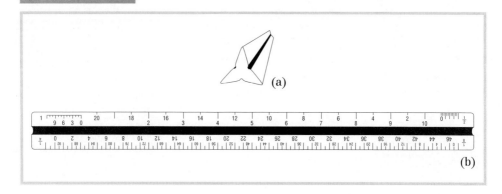

(a)

(b)

FIGURES D.3

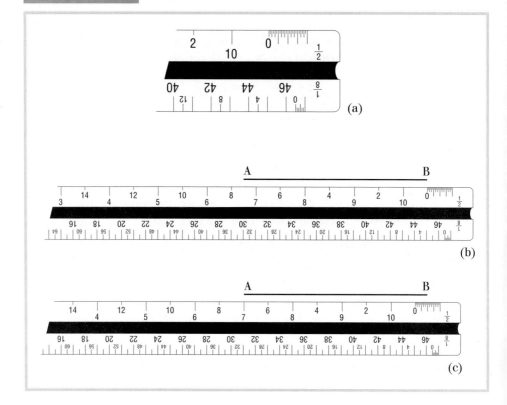

(a)

(b)

(c)

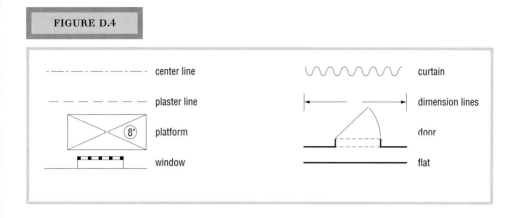

FIGURE D.4

The *center line (CL)* and *plaster line (PL)* or *set line (SL)* are the reference lines for measuring the placement of all scenery. The center line divides the stage from front to back; the plaster line intersects the center line at the back (or upstage of) the **proscenium wall.** The set line is the most downstage point of the scenery. Figure D-5 illustrates the four standard types of stages or performance spaces. They will vary in size and shape from one theatre to another.

Plotting corners on the ground plan is the next step in the process. First, be sure a center line and plaster line are marked on the drawing. Next, determine which corners of the scenery need to be measured in order to transfer the drawing (see Figure D-6).

There are two different methods for plotting corners. The conventional method (see Figure D-7) is to determine the position of each corner of scenery by measuring its distance from the center line and plaster line as follows:

1. Draw a horizontal line from the corner to the center line, leaving an open place in the line for entering the distance between the two points.
2. Draw a vertical line from the same corner to the plaster line, leaving an open space in the line for entering the distance between the two points.

The alternative method (see Figure D-8) for plotting corners is as follows:

1. Measure a point on the plaster line beginning at the center line and ending at least two feet from the proscenium wall. From the center line, measure the same point on the other side of the stage.
2. Measure each corner of the drawing from both of these points.

Transferring the drawing from the ground plan to the rehearsal/stage floor requires assistance. Bring your ASM and a PA or other volunteer. If this is your first time, ask the scene designer or technical director to supervise, at

FIGURE D.5

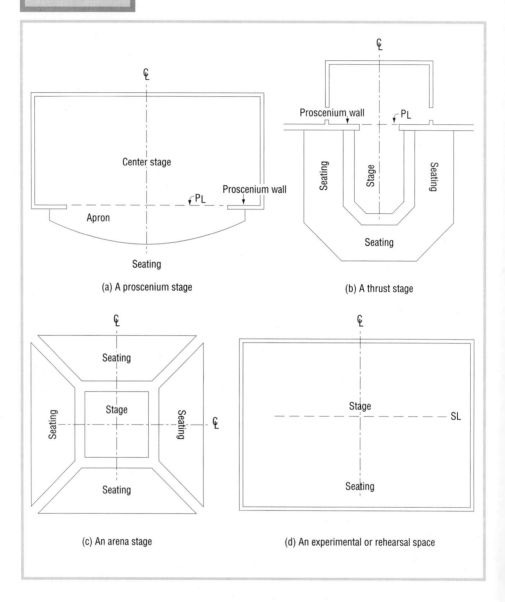

(a) A proscenium stage

(b) A thrust stage

(c) An arena stage

(d) An experimental or rehearsal space

least for the first few measurements. Bring two twenty-five- or thirty-foot tape measures, the drawing, your scale ruler, a piece of chalk, a roll of 1-inch masking tape, a roll of one-half-inch masking tape, and (if it is a complicated drawing) a bottle of aspirin.

Use the 1-inch masking tape to represent flats or vertical scenery and the

FIGURE D.6

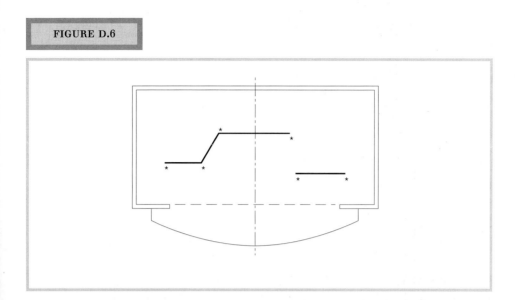

one-half-inch masking tape to represent platforms and steps. If you have more than one ground plan because of changes in scenery, you may use a different color of tape for each drawing.

Get a table to put the drawing on. Place it downstage center where you can observe the taping from a logical viewpoint. Have your assistants do all the measuring and taping while you call out the measurements.

FIGURE D.7

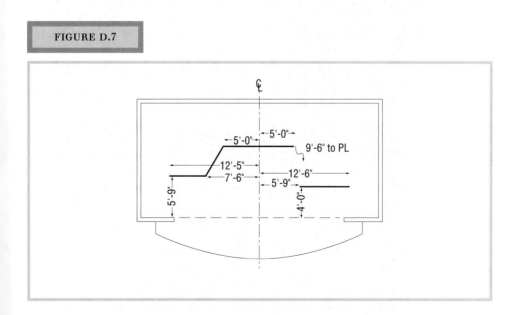

FIGURE D.8

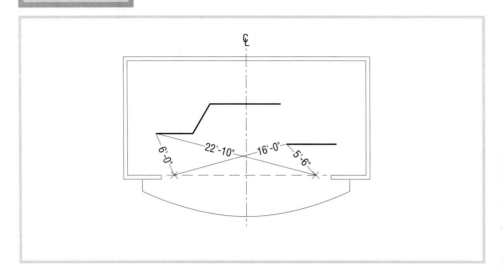

Next, be sure the center line and plaster line are clearly marked. If you are transferring a ground plan to a stage, these lines may already be taped. If you are taping a ground plan in a rehearsal hall, you will probably have to create your own center line and plaster line with tape or by popping a chalk line. If you use a chalk line, be sure to mop the chalk up after the taping session is finished. Otherwise, it will be mopped up by actors' clothing and skin.

The *conventional method:*

1. Plot each corner on the floor as you did on the ground plan, substituting the measuring tape for the scale ruler. Have two people using tapes, one person measuring from the center line and the other from the plaster line. For greater accuracy, **anchor** a measuring tape to the center line, beginning at its intersection with the plaster line.
2. At the point where the two tapes meet, make an X with a piece of chalk (see Figure D-9a).
3. Plot the next corner that connects with the first one; then tape the floor between the two chalk marks (see Figure D-9b).

The *alternative method:*

1. Using the measuring tape, mark two points on the plaster line equidistant from the center line as shown on the ground plan (see Figure D-10). All measurements will be made from these two points.
2. Either attach the "dummy" end of a measuring tape at each of these two marks or (if you have the manpower) have two assistants hold the tapes

FIGURE D.9

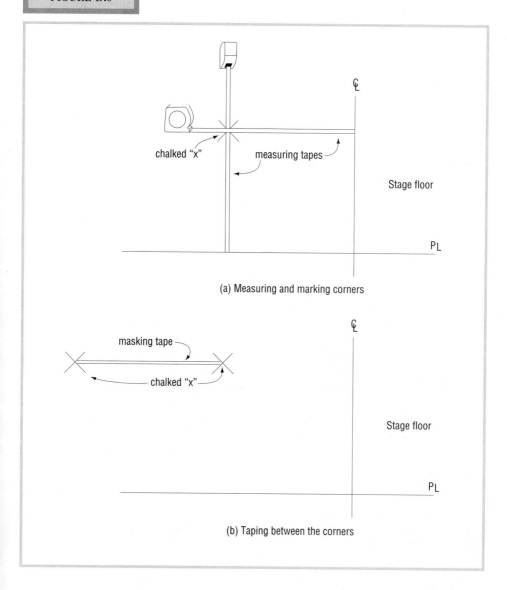

(a) Measuring and marking corners

(b) Taping between the corners

on the marks. When you call out the measurements, the person(s) holding the measuring tapes will find the spot where the two measurements meet. It is actually more efficient and accurate to drill a small hole in the end of the measuring tape and nail it to the floor, leaving space for it to swivel. The tape will remain in the precise position and you can call out the measurements while a second person finds the converging points and a third person helps lay down the masking tape.

FIGURE D.10

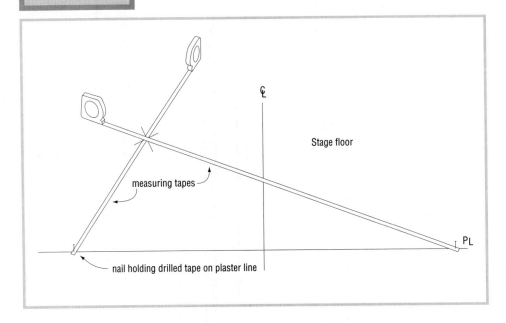

This alternative method is less commonly used only because fewer people know about it, but it is a faster and more precise way to transfer the drawing. You should be familiar with both methods so you can use either.

Taping doors, windows, counters, appliances, and so on must also be done in order for the actors to find their entrances, exits, and definition for their acting areas (see Figure D-11). It is also important to identify on which side a door is hinged as well as whether it opens into or out of the room. Since door and window openings are usually built into walls, you can locate their posi-

FIGURE D.11

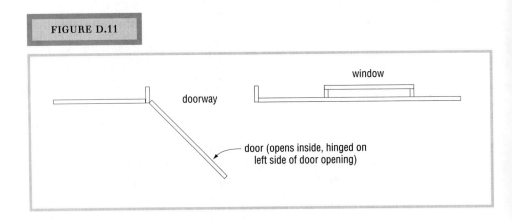

tions by measuring them on the wall line rather than plotting two corners. The same is true for counters, appliances, and other items that are against a wall. Do not bother taping moveable pieces of furniture or other set props. Bring in those rehearsal props that the director will need to make a final decision with regard to their placement. Once the director decides, spike their positions with tape (see Appendix E).

> *NOTE: The sample design used in this appendix is very simple. Some designs are this simple, but most are not. Remember to get assistance in determining what each line in the ground plan represents and transfer only those that are needed for blocking. Have the designer check your work. Otherwise, you might leave out a structure that will destroy the director's blocking once the scenery is in place. For example, a fireplace hearth can be an obstacle that forces an actor downstage, or it can be another level for the director to use.*

PROP TABLES

Tables used to hold props backstage are usually the standard six-by-two-foot tables with fold-up legs. If entrances are made from both sides of the stage with props carried by actors or crew members, there should be a prop table convenient to each entrance. Some shows are very "prop heavy" requiring several tables per side. If there is limited space backstage, the prop tables may have to be located in the hall or a space near an entrance to the stage.

Each prop table should be covered with paper. The paper may be newsprint, butcher paper, or brown shipping paper. Use masking tape to attach it to the table. Place all of the props on the tables in positions that will make them easy to locate.

> Example: You may choose to place smaller items in the front where they are easier to see; or you may put things in the order in which they will be used.

After the props are placed on the tables, use a marker pen to draw around them on the paper; then write the name of the object inside the drawn shape.

This allows you to check the tables before each rehearsal or performance to see that everything is in place. A missing prop will be very obvious. It also identifies where a prop needs to be returned after its use.

SPIKING PROPS

Spiking props means identifying where set props (furniture or other move-able pieces of scenery) are to be placed on the stage. After the director has defined exactly where he/she wants a set prop, use one-half-inch masking tape or colored tape coded for each scene change and tape the stage floor at

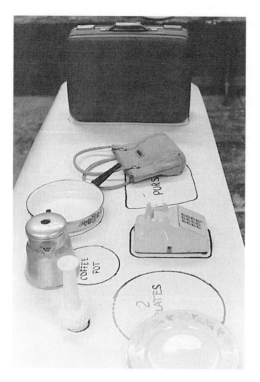

Props, their outlines drawn and labeled on paper covering the table, can be easily returned to their proper place or noticed if missing. (Photo by J. B. Alston)

Masking tape marks the correct location for a set prop. (Photo by J. B. Alston)

the upstage corners of the object. Use two pieces of tape to create a corner or shape for the object to fit into.

SPIKING SCENERY

The same method is used for spiking scenery (mobile vertical units and platforms) if scenery changes are made during a show or if the stage must be cleared following each performance. When the scenery is in place, tape upstage of each corner or other strategic location. If you are using color-coded tape, coordinate the color for the scenery with the color used for the set props for each scene.

> *NOTE: Use as little tape as possible without sacrificing clarity for the stage crew. Too much tape can be confusing for the crew and can become a distraction for the audience. Too much tape also can aggravate a designer who perhaps has spent much time creating a special look for the floor of the set.*

NUMBERING AND CALLING CUES | F

The stage manager calls the show (gives technical cues) from a station. This station may be located backstage (in the wings) or in the control booth (usually opposite the stage, above and behind the audience).

VERBAL CUES

The communication system through which you speak to the technicians operating lights, sound, fly system, and so on will include headsets. Your headsets may be attached to a power source limiting range of movement, or they may be battery operated, giving complete freedom of movement. There may be one channel, allowing everyone with a headset to hear all called cues and to hear one another's responses; there may be multiple channels allowing all technicians to hear you, but not to hear each other; or you may have one-on-one communication with each technician.

These differences in the communication system will affect the way you number and call cues. If you have one channel for calling cues, you can number all cues (regardless of type) consecutively, or you may choose to do this if you have multiple channels but keep the lines open so that all technicians hear all calls.

Example: cue 1, lights (house lights up, work
lights out, preset lights up)
cue 2, sound (preshow music begins)
cue 3, lights (house to half)
cue 4, sound (preshow music begins slow fade)
cue 5, lights (house and preset lights crossfade with lights for
scene 1)

If a technician is listening to all cues being called, he/she can be more pre-pared for each cue if they are numbered consecutively (as above) rather than being numbered as follows:

Example: cue 23, lights
              cue 5, sound
              cue 2, followspot
              cue 24, lights
              cue 25, lights
              cue 6, sound

However, if your communication system has a separate channel for each technician, it would be simpler to divide cues into categories or types, number them individually (as in the example above), and communicate only with the technician being cued.

In preparation for the execution of a technical cue, you will give a *warning* at least 1 minute before time for the cue, a *stand-by* a few lines of dialogue be-fore the cue, and a *go* at the precise moment the execution of the cue should begin.

Example: light cue 23, warning
              sound cue 6, stand by
              sound cue 6, go
              light cue 23, stand by
              light cue 23, go

If cues are to happen simultaneously (as they often do), you can group them in a call.

Example: light 23 and sound 6, warning
              light 23 and sound 6, stand by
              light 23 and sound 6, go.
or: cue 23, light and sound, warning
              cue 23, light and sound, stand by
              cue 23, go

NOTE: *"Stand by" is sometimes not used. If the show has many cues, it may only add to the confusion.*

RESPONSES TO CUES

To assure the stage manager that a called cue was received, the technician should respond with the following:

light cue 23, warned
light cue 23, standing
light cue 23, completed

> *NOTE: Once again, if there are many cues happening simultaneously or one after the other, responses may only confuse you and your crew. Determine how many responses are necessary for your production to run smoothly amd precisely.*

CUE LIGHTS

In the best of all worlds, you will have a console from which you call cues. This console will have a panel of light switches that allows you to cue actors, crew members, and some technicians with colored lights placed at entrances or operator positions.

When the light is turned on, it replaces "warning" and "stand by"; When the light is turned off, it replaces the "go" cue. This is especially helpful when an action (by an actor), rather than a line of dialogue, cues an entrance. The actor or crew member may not be in a position to see the action. It can also be necessary if the cue is a sound which is difficult to hear from the entrance position.

The light switches must be clearly labeled with corresponding labels written into the cueing script.

RELAYED CUES

In place of cue lights and an adequate supply of headsets, the ASM must relay cues from the wings. A raised arm might be an adequate warning and stand-by signal, and a lowered arm might be an adequate go signal. Find a method which works with your crew positions and backstage visibility.

BACKSTAGE CUES

Your console may also be equipped with a paging system that allows you to call warnings in dressing rooms and the green room. Otherwise, the ASM or a production assistant will be responsible for relaying "time calls" (30 minutes, 15 minutes, 10 minutes, 5 minutes, *places*).

MUSICAL CUES

If you are stage managing a musical play, an opera, a ballet, or simply a play with music, you may have to call cues based on a note in the score. This requires the ability to read music. It is a skill you should have if you are going to work with music.

Some directors argue that they do not want the SM's head down, following music, rather than watching the effect of the cues or the action on stage. Whenever possible, base your cues on visual action (such as dance steps) which allows you to keep an eye on the stage.

CUE FOLLOW-UP

Always look or listen to verify that each cue has been properly executed. If a mistake is made (the wrong lights raised, the wrong piece of scenery lowered, etc.), you must decide the best course of action that will draw the least attention to the mistake without compromising the scene.

> *NOTE: You must call all cues, even if they are relayed by someone else. Never allow technicians (especially lights or sound) to operate on visual cues. The timing is critical and you are responsible for it being accurate. The sound technician or board operator may have been with the show for only a few rehearsals, but you have been with it from the beginning and must follow the script in anticipation of line changes, accidents that affect the order of action, and so on. In other words, you have to be ready to troubleshoot at all times and that may affect the timing and order of cues.*

GLOSSARY

Acoustics   The sound-producing qualities in a performance space.

Act curtain   (see **Curtain**)

Acting area   The space used by actors during a performance. This may include the aisles, a side stage in front of the proscenium wall, seats in the auditorium, or any place where the action of the play might occur.

Ad-lib   Any line of dialogue or action that is used to cover an error such as a dropped line, a late entrance, a missing prop, and so on.

AEA   Actors' Equity Association, the union for stage actors and stage managers.

AFTRA   American Federation of Television and Radio Artists, the union for radio and television performers.

Amateur   One who participates in a theatrical production for personal pleasure rather than for professional or financial profit.

Amphitheatre   An outdoor oval or circular performing area with rising tiers of seats.

Anchor   To attach or weight an object so that it will not move.

Angel   A financial investor in a theatrical production.

Antagonist   (also called the "villain") A character in a play who is an adversary or an opponent to the protagonist.

Anticipate   To react to a line of dialogue or other cue before it occurs.

Apprentice   A person who works in the theatre for the learning experience, often for the opportunity to work with a particular professional. This position is usually unpaid.

Apron   The part of the stage that extends in front of the proscenium wall.

Arbor   (also called "carriage" or "cradle") The frame which houses the weights in a counterweight system used to fly scenery.

Arena stage   (also called "theatre in the round") Any theatre which provides seating on all sides of the acting area.

Arm   A short batten supporting a tall narrow curtain usually used to create wing space.

Artistic director   The person responsible for making major artistic decisions in a production company.

Asbestos curtain   A fire-retardant curtain located upstage of the grand drape.

Aside   Dialogue addressed directly to the audience, which other characters on stage cannot hear.

ASM   Assistant stage manager, part of the stage management staff.

ATPAM   Association of Theatrical Press Agents and Managers, the union for theatre publicists and house managers.

Audition   A performance before producers, directors, or others for the purpose of being cast in a production.

Auditorium   (also called the "house") The seating area from which the audience watches the play.

Backlight   To focus lights on the backs of actors to highlight and separate them from the scenery.

Backing   Flats, drops, or curtains placed behind openings to mask the audience's view of the backstage areas.

Backstage   (also called "offstage") Any part of the stage outside of the acting area or any part of the theatre other than the acting area and the house (foyer and auditorium).

Barndoor   Metal flaps placed on a spotlight to reduce and shape the beam of light.

Batten   A *pipe batten* is a length of metal hung horizontally above the acting area to hold curtains, scenery, and so on. A *wooden batten* is usually attached to the top and bottom of a drop which is then hung on a pipe batten.

Beam   A position in the ceiling of an auditorium where spotlights can be hung.

Bit part   (also called a "walk-on") A small role with few or no lines.

Black box   (theatre) A large open room, often painted black, used for flexible placement of audience and performers.

Blackout   An extinguishing of the lights on the entire acting area, often to end a scene or act.

Blacks   Black curtains.

Blocking   Planning the movement of actors in the acting area.

Blocking notation   A written or symbolic description of the actors' movements that is recorded in the actors' scripts and the stage manager's production book.

Blueline   (also called the "diazo process") To copy drawings made on vellum tracing paper; the lines are usually blue, sometimes black.

Blueprint   A drawing reproduction in which the background is blue and the lines are white.

Board operator   The technician who controls the lights (runs the light board) during technical rehearsals and performances.

Boards   The stage.

Book   1. The script. 2. In musicals, the libretto without the music. 3. To fold hinged flats together like a book.

Book ceiling   (see **Ceiling**)

Border   Wide short drops that are hung on battens and used to mask the fly space and any scenery or lights hung there.

Border lights (also called "strip lights") Rows of lights mounted in a metal frame, used for general lighting or to light a scrim or drop.

Boxes   The seats on the sides of the auditorium; boxes usually have separate entrances and seat six to eight people.

Box set   A traditional interior set with three walls.

Break a leg   The traditional way of wishing an actor a good performance without saying "good luck" (considered to be bad luck).

Breakaway   Scenery, props, or costumes that disappear, break, or change form in view of the audience.

Break character   For an actor to lose concentration or say or do something that is not consistent with the character being portrayed.

Bring up   (also called "dim in" or "dim up") To increase the intensity of the lights.

Brush-up rehearsals   Rehearsals used to return a show to its original blocking and stage business, which may have changed during a long run or a long absence.

Build   An acceleration of tempo or intensity of a performance.

Bump it   To hit the floor with flown scenery in order to trim or level it.

Bump up   A sudden increase in the intensity of lights.

Bury the show   To strike the show after the last performance.

Cable   1. A flexible insulated wire for conducting current for technical effects and communication systems. 2. A wire rope used to support heavy pieces of scenery.

Call   1. A notice of the time of rehearsal or performance, placed on the callboard. 2. A warning to all actors for the beginning of an act (half-hour call, 15-minute call, 5-minute call). 3. To give cues to technicians and actors, usually done by the stage manager (calling the show).

Callboard   A bulletin board hung near the stage or rehearsal space for all announcements related to the production.

Cast   1. The performers in a play 2. The act of selecting performers for roles in a play.

Cat walk   A balcony or ledge near the light battens (electrics) used by electricians to hang and focus lights.

Ceiling   A structure used at the top of the scenery to suggest part or all of a ceiling: *book ceiling*–two hinged flats stored in a "booked" (face-to-face) position, then lowered and opened to create a ceiling for the scenery; *roll ceiling*–fabric attached to two battens (front and back) which can be rolled for storage and transportation.

Center stage   The middle of the acting area.

Chalk line   A tool used to make a line on the stage or scenery using string and powdered chalk.

Chew the scenery   To rant and rave onstage.

Choreographer   The person responsible for creating dance sequences in a musical production.

Chorus   A group of singers, dancers, or speakers who perform in unison.

Clamp   A tool used for joining lighting instruments to battens, step units to platforms, and so on.

Claque   An audience member paid to begin applause at specific times.

Clear please   1. An order to remove props or to leave the stage. 2. A warning that the curtain is going up.

Climax   The point of highest interest or intensity in a scene or the major turning point in the action when the theme of the play is revealed.

Clip cues   To interrupt a performer's lines before the cue phrase is completed.

Clip lights   Low-wattage blue lights that can be clipped backstage to give needed illumination for movement of actors and crew.

Cold reading   To audition by reading from a script with no opportunity to read or rehearse the lines.

Color medium   A transparent material used in front of a light source to project a colored beam of light.

Come down   To move downstage, toward the audience.

Comps   (complimentary tickets) Production tickets available to the members of a company at no cost.

Contact sheet   A list of names, phone numbers, and addresses of all performers, staff, and crew associated with a production.

Control booth   The room in which light and sound equipment are operated.

Costume designer   The person responsible for planning the style, color, fabric, and character details for the clothing in a play.

Counterweight system   A method of raising and lowering scenery that involves the adjustment of weight in the arbor to match the weight of the scenery on the batten.

Cover   1. To block the audience's view of an actor, a piece of scenery, or a prop. 2. To adapt one's lines and actions to replace a missing actor's character.

Cradle   (see **Arbor**)

Crash box   A box of broken glass or the objects that create a specific sound effect when shaken.

Crepe hair   Artificial hair used for beards, moustaches, bushy eyebrows.

Crisis   The turning point in a play.

Cross   A blocking command to move from one place to another on the stage.

Crossover   A passageway behind the scenery used to get from one side of the stage to the other.

Cue   A prearranged signal given to actors or crew which can be visual (a movement or a change in lights) or audible (a spoken word or a sound effect).

Cue light   A light that signals crew members or actors to prepare for an action when it is turned on and signals them to "go" when it is turned off.

Cue sheet   A list of numbered cues used to call the show.

Cue-to-cue   A run-through of the performance with actors skipping in dialogue and action from one technical cue to the next in order to set levels for lights and sound.

Curtains   Draperies that can be used to hide the stage, scenery, fly space, and backstage from the audience: *main curtain* (also called "grand drape," "front curtain," "house curtain," "act curtain," "flag," or "rag"); *midstage curtain; borders* (also called "teasers"); and *legs* (also called "tormentors").

Curtain line   1. The last line of a scene, which is the cue for the curtain to close. 2. An imaginary line where the main curtain touches the floor.

Curtain time   Time set for the play to begin.

Cut   To eliminate an action or a line from a script.

Cut line   A line that holds the asbestos curtain and is cut or released in case of a fire.

Cyc   Slang for *cyclorama;* a term sometimes used to refer to a *scrim* (although they are not the same).

Cyclorama   An unseamed expanse of light blue or white fabric enclosing the acting area on three sides. It can be used to represent sky and/or as a screen on which symbolic or mood enhancing colors or images can be projected.

Dance captain   The person who helps teach, rehearse, and maintain dance choreography.

Dark night   An evening when the theatre is not open to the public.

Dead spot   An area onstage that is not adequately lighted.

Dim   To decrease the intensity of lights on stage using a rheostat or dimmer.

Dimmer   An electrical unit used to regulate current, increasing or decreasing intensity.

Dimmerboard   (also called "switchboard") Panel of dimmers and switches from which stage lighting is controlled.

Director   The person responsible for interpreting the script, blocking the action, and coordinating the various artistic aspects of the production.

Dolly   A low platform on wheels used in moving heavy objects.

Dome   A plaster cyclorama.

Downstage   Toward the audience.

Draw curtain   (also called a "traveller") A curtain on a track which allows it to be opened from the center to each side.

Dress parade   An opportunity for the

director and costumer to see costumes on actors and under lights prior to dress rehearsal.

Drop A large piece of unframed fabric which suggests the environment of the play.

Dresser A crew member that assists an actor in and out of costume.

Dress rehearsal A rehearsal that includes costumes.

Dropped lines Dialogue that an actor did not give.

Dry tech The same as a cue-to-cue without actors. The stage manager, technicians, and stage crew rehearse calling and carrying out technical cues.

Dumps Tickets returned, not sold.

Electrician (see **Board Operator**)

Elevator stage A part of the stage floor that can be raised or lowered by a hydraulic system.

Ensemble Performers or performers and technicians working together as a single unit to achieve a common goal.

Epilogue A speech or scene performed after the end of the play.

Equity (see **AEA**)

Escape stairs The stairs that actors use for upper level entrances and exits; escape stairs are not seen by the audience.

Exteriors Scenery that represents outdoor spaces.

Extra (also called "supernumerary") Performer without lines who contributes atmosphere as bystander, passerby, part of a crowd, and so on.

Fade A gradual raising (*fade in*) or lowering (*fade out*) of the intensity of lights.

False proscenium A decorated extension, placed upstage of the structural proscenium. It is designed for the production to decrease the size of the proscenium opening or to provide additional atmosphere which may suggest period, style, mood, and so on.

Feedback Noise from a speaker usually caused by a microphone getting too close to the speaker.

Fight director The person responsible for choreographing combat on stage.

Final dress (rehearsal) The last rehearsal before opening night, treated exactly like a regular performance, often including an invited audience.

Fire curtain A curtain that will not burn and that is lowered in case of a fire in order to contain the flames on stage, thereby protecting the audience.

Flag (see **Curtain**)

Flash pot A small box that creates an explosion and smoke through the electrical ignition of gun powder.

Flat A two-dimensional unit of scenery made of a wooden frame covered by muslin or luan.

Flies (also called "fly space") The space above the stage into which scenery, lights, or curtains can be raised or *flown.*

Float To lower a standing fabric-covered flat to a face-down position by putting a foot on the lower rail and allowing it to fall to the floor. The fabric slows the fall through air resistance.

Floodlight An instrument which projects a large diffused beam of light for general illumination of an area.

Floor cloth (also called "ground cloth") A fabric covering for the stage.

Floor plan A technical drawing that indicates the position of scenery and set props on stage.

Fly To raise scenery, lights, or curtains into the fly space. In some productions such as *Peter Pan*, actors are flown.

Fly deck (also called "fly gallery" and "fly floor") A narrow balcony beside the ropes that are used to operate the fly system.

Fly man   The person who operates the fly system from the fly floor.

Focus   1. To aim and shutter lighting instruments. 2. Where the audience's attention is directed during a scene. This can be accomplished by position of actors, stage business, or lights.

Follow spot   A lighting instrument which is manually controlled to provide a beam of light for a moving performer.

Footiron   A brace on the bottom rail of a flat which is used to attach it to the stage floor.

Footlights   A strip of lights anchored to the stage floor downstage of the curtain.

Foul   To tangle flown objects such as scenery or lights in the flies.

Fourth wall   (also called "imaginary wall") The hypothetical wall through which the audience views the play.

French scene   A division of a script based on the entrance or exit of a character or characters.

Fresnel   A lighting instrument named for the person who developed its lens. It is used to provide a beam of light with soft edges.

Front   The area that includes the auditorium and lobby of the theatre.

Front of house   Usually refers to staff positions related to the business of theatre such as house management, box office, and so on.

Front curtain   (see **Curtain**)

Full   The highest intensity of sound or lights.

Full dress   A dress rehearsal with costumes, makeup, wigs, and any other accessories that complete the visual characters.

Full tech   All technical effects are incorporated into the rehearsal.

Gagging   The unauthorized improvisation or ad-libbing of lines by an actor.

Gallery   The highest balcony in the theatre.

Gang   1. To attach similar objects. 2. To group dimmers and move them as one.

Gel   A transparent color medium used for spotlights, originally made from gelatin.

Gel frame   A metal or cardboard frame used for holding gel in a slot at the front of a spotlight.

Ghost   A light that leaks from an instrument and spills where it is not wanted.

Ghost light   A light onstage when the theatre is closed; used to prevent an accident (such as falling off the stage in the dark).

Give stage   To change position onstage in order to make space for a cross by another actor or to give focus to another actor.

Go   The order to execute a cue.

Go up on lines   To forget lines.

Gobo   A metal disk with punched pattern that is used in a spotlight to project the pattern on a scrim, flat, or other surface, enhancing or replacing scenery.

Good show   Another way of saying "good luck."

Gopher   A production assistant who may be asked to "go for" many things.

Grand drape   (see **Curtain**)

Grand valance   The first border in front of the front curtain.

Green room   The lounge where actors wait to go onstage or where they meet the public following the performance.

Grid   A framework of beams above the stage used to support the flying system rigging.

Grip   A stagehand who helps move scenery.

Ground cloth   (see **Floor cloth**)

Ground plan   (see **Floor plan**)

Ground row   1. Strip lights positioned on the floor to light the lower half of a drop, scrim, or cyc. 2. Low masking in front of strip lights, machinery, and so on that may be shaped and/or painted to suggest the style or location of the play.

Half-hour   The 30-minute warning to cast and crews before the curtain goes up.

Hanger iron   A metal strap with a ring used in hanging scenery.

Hardware   Tickets for standing room.

Heads up   The order to watch for overhead activity that may be hazardous.

Hold   To maintain a position without moving.

Hold book   To cue actors and take blocking and technical notes during rehearsals.

Hoofer   A dancer.

Horseplay   Rough physical actions not appropriate to the activity at hand.

House   Any part of the theatre that accommodates the needs of the audience (foyer, auditorium, box office, restrooms, and so on).

House lights   The instruments that provide lights for the audience in the auditorium.

IATSE   International Alliance of Theatrical and Stage Employees, the union for stagehands.

Improvisation   To spontaneously create a physical and/or verbal scene, often used as an acting exercise or in auditions.

Intensity   1. The brightness or dimness of lights. 2. The emotional tension in a character or a scene.

Interiors   Scenery that represents indoor spaces.

IPA   International Phonetic Alphabet, symbols used to represent sounds for accurate pronunciation and stress.

Jack   A triangular brace attached to the back of standing scenery or ground rows.

Jacknife stage   A platform on casters, attached to a pivot point so it can be rolled onstage or off (usually two are used, one on each upstage side of the proscenium opening).

Jog   A narrow flat no more than two feet wide.

Jury   An opening night audience.

Keylight   The main light on an actor or acting area.

Kill   To eliminate a piece of scenery or props or to stop a technical effect.

Lash   to attach two flats with a lashline (sash cord) wrapped around a lashcleat (metal hook).

Leg   A long narrow curtain located on the sides of the stage and used to mask offstage right and offstage left and to create entrances.

Leko   Any lighting instrument with an ellipsoidal reflector.

Levels   Platforms, ramps, risers, or any change in the floor of the stage that elevates the actors or scenery.

Light batten   (see **Electric**)

Light plot   Plan for light changes and cues for a production from preset to curtain call.

Light towers   (also called "light trees") Poles on the sides of the stage to which spotlights can be attached to provide extra or *side* lighting (especially important for dance).

Lines   Dialogue in a script.

Load-in   The movement of scenery, props, and costumes (from a truck or shop) to the theatre.

Load-out   The movement of scenery, props, and costumes (to a truck or storage spaces) from the theatre.

Manager   There may be many managers in a company or only one, depending on the budget and the size of the staff. Unlike stage managers, their responsibilities are associated with the business of theatre, not the artistic or technical aspects. Producer (responsible for entire production), business manager (responsible for budget and contracts), company manager (responsible for the company, especially on tour), house manager (responsible for the physical theatre and audience) and personal manager (responsible for an actor) are some of the titles of personnel in this category.

Main curtain   (see **Curtain**)

Mask   To cover an object or space in order to prevent the audience from seeing it.

Masking flats   Framed scenery used to prevent the audience from seeing into the wings or backstage.

Mugging   The use of excessive, exaggerated facial expressions on stage.

Music director   The person responsible for interpreting the musical score for voices and instruments.

Muslin   The most commonly used fabric for covering flats.

Notices   Reviews by critics.

Off-book   A point in the rehearsal process when the actor has learned all lines and can put the script (book) down.

Offstage   The area outside of the acting space.

Onstage   The acting space.

Open cold   To perform for critics without first performing out of town or for a preview or invited audience.

Orchestra   The lowest seating area, nearest the stage.

Orchestra pit   A recessed space in front of the stage that is used for musicians.

PA   Production assistant, responsible to ASM in rehearsals and performances.

Pace   (tempo) The timing of a speech, action, or scene.

Pan   An unfavorable review by a critic.

Paper tech   The first technical rehearsal in which the crews meet with the tech director, the stage

manager, and sometimes the director. Cues are listed and numbered on paper.

Patch panel   A station where dimmers can be interconnected.

Picking up the cues   Shortening the time between lines or business.

Places   The term used by the stage manager to call actors to their entrances or waiting positions for the opening of an act or scene.

Plant   An actor placed in the audience to participate in the action or to respond to the action on stage.

Platform   A portable weight-bearing unit that adds variety to the stage levels and can represent a separate space. For example, one platformed area may represent the kitchen while the stage floor represents the parlor or an outside garden.

Practical   Something on stage (scenery or prop) that will function the way it would in real life. For example, a practical window is one that will be raised or opened; a practical lamp is one that will be lit.

Preset   To position props or costumes on stage prior to the opening of the act or scene.

Preset lights   Those lights on the scenery when the front curtain is not used before the show begins.

Preview   A performance given before the publicized opening night, often for an invited audience.

Producer   The person(s) responsible for obtaining the script, finances, and personnel for a production. This may be an individual in the profession, a committee in a community organization, or a department in a university. The role may broaden to include other management responsibilities with the exception of stage management.

Production book   (also called "Promptbook") The notebook which houses the stage manager's script as well as all forms, notes, blocking, and so on relevant to the running of rehearsals or performances.

Production log   The diary of the production from the first rehearsal to the last performance.

Prompt   1. On time. 2. To give a line to an actor who has dropped, changed, or gone up on a line.

Promptbook   (see **Production book**)

Prop box   Large box, preferably on casters, that is kept offstage for prop storage and/or touring.

Props   (Properties) Objects used in a play: *hand props* (objects brought on or handled by actors such as a cane, a pipe, a vase of flowers); *set props* (moveable pieces of scenery such as furniture, a tree stump, a wagon); and *dress* or *trim props* (objects that decorate the scenery such as curtains on a window, a mirror on the wall, a lantern on a porch post.

Prop table   An offstage table on which props are placed to be picked up by actors to carry onstage or by crew members to preset during a scene change.

Proscenium doors   The side doors between the audience and the proscenium through which actors may enter or exit the forestage or stage apron.

Proscenium opening   The rectangular or arched opening in the proscenium wall through which the audience views the play.

Proscenium stage   The most common stage architecture in America and Europe, it has a wall with a rectangular opening through which the audience watches the performance.

Proscenium wall   The wall in a traditional theatre that separates the audience from the actors or acting area.

Protagonist   The hero or heroine of a play who is in conflict with the antagonist.

Pyrotechnician   A licensed individual who is responsible for the supervision of all effects that involve fire or explosives.

Quick change   A fast costume change that does not allow time to go to a dressing room.

Quick change booth   A temporary dressing space set up backstage to allow privacy for fast costume changes.

Quick study   The ability to memorize lines and blocking easily.

Rag   (see **Curtain**)

Raked stage   Angling the stage floor so that the downstage area is lower than the upstage area.

Raking   Angling anything on stage to make it more visible to the audience. For example, a bed may be raked with the head higher than the foot so a reclining actor may be seen more easily.

Read-through   An early rehearsal in which the script is read and discussed from beginning to end.

Repertory   A group of productions that are performance ready. A rep company can perform a different show each night of a given period rather than the same show every night.

Reprise   To repeat a musical number.

Return   A flat placed at the downstage end of a wall flat to support and mask the end of the flat and provide additional backstage masking.

Reveal   (also called **Return**) Material used to suggest structural thickness such as in an archway.

Rhythm   1. A musical term that refers to a regulated pattern of sound. 2. An acting or directing term that refers to divisions or patterns in plot, dialogue, or action. 3. An element of visual design that can be used for scenery, costumes, and lights.

Ring down   To close the front curtain.

Ring up   To raise the front curtain.

Risers   (see **Levels**)

Road show   A production that is toured to several theatres.

Road apple   A touring performer.

Roundels   Round glass color media used in ground or strip lights.

Royalty   Payment to a playwright or composer for each performance of his/her script.

Run   The number of performances of a production.

Running crew   The technical crew needed to operate a production.

Running order   The order of scenes and music in a production.

Run-through   A rehearsal in which the entire play is performed without stopping, except for scene changes or act breaks.

Runway   The extension of a narrow stage into the audience area.

SAG   Screen Actors Guild, the union for film actors.

Scene   A division of a script usually based on changes in time, location, action, or characters.

Scene breakdown   A division of a script into rehearsal units which are appropriate in length, characters, and completion of an action.

Scene designer   The person responsible for planning the style, colors, textures, and arrangement of the physical environment for a play.

Scene dock   The backstage area designated as a holding place for scenery that will be used in the play.

Scenery   The environment created for a play.

Scrim   A fabric that can be used in place of a cyclorama to represent sky or as a screen for projected color or images. It has translucent qualities so that the audience can see through it when it is lit from behind.

Set   (see **Scenery**)

Shift   To change scenery or props between scenes or acts.

Shift plot   The plan (who moves what to where and when) for a shift.

Shops   Spaces for construction of scenery, props, or costumes.

Side   Part of a script containing only those pages that include the lines of one character, usually prepared for actors with few lines.

Sign in   To sign an attendance sheet to establish presence for a rehearsal, performance, or work session.

Sight lines   Imaginary lines that define the area onstage that can be seen by all of the audience.

SM   Stage manager, responsible for running rehearsals, production meetings, and performances.

Snatch lines   Ropes or chains used to attach scenery to battens.

Sound designer   The person responsible for planning, creating, and setting up the technical equipment needed for executing the sound effects in a production.

Sound effects   Sounds made offstage that are designed to enhance the production.

Sound technician   The person responsible for executing the sound cues during a performance.

Special effects   Unusual effects such as blood, rain, illusions.

Spike   To tape the position of the set props on the stage floor.

Spill   Light in inappropriate places due to errors in focusing or shuttering.

Spotlight   An instrument used to light actors and scenery.

Stage   The performance space.

Stage brace   An adjustable brace used for supporting scenery.

Stage business   Activities or mannerisms which an actor develops to help communicate the personality of a character.

Stage cable   An electrical conductor with a thick covering, which makes it very durable.

Stage combat Choreographed action that gives the illusion of fighting.

Stage directions Instructions in the script which describe actions of characters. Unless they are necessary for the dialogue to make sense, the director is not bound to them.

Stagehand Backstage workers/helpers.

Stage left The acting area to the actor's left when standing in the center of the stage and facing the audience.

Stage picture The visual effect of the arrangement of the actors on stage.

Stage right The acting area to the actor's right when standing in the center of the stage and facing the audience.

Stage weights Rectangular metal blocks used primarily in the counterweight system but also useful in weighting anything onstage, especially in theatres that restrict the use of screws or nails in the stage floor.

Stage whisper An actor's use of breathiness with voice in order to suggest a whisper, but one that can be heard by the entire audience.

Stand by An instruction from the stage manager to a technician to be ready to execute a cue.

Standby (see **Understudy**)

Stock A company that performs one play while rehearsing the next one; usually performs one play per week for a limited season.

Stock scenery Stored scenery (often standardized in size) that can be reused.

Strike 1. To eliminate or put away. 2. To clear the stage of scenery and props.

Strip lights Connected rows of lights that provide general illumination and usually are positioned at the top and bottom of a cyclorama, scrim, or painted drop.

Supernumerary (see **Extra**)

Switchboard (see **Dimmerboard**)

Take it out A request to raise scenery into the fly space.

Take stage To move into an area of focus while other actors *give stage*.

Teaser (see **Curtain**)

Technical director An individual who supervises the building of scenery and set props and oversees technical rehearsals.

Technical rehearsal (tech) A rehearsal that includes technical effects such as lights, sound, scenery, and so on.

Technician (also called "technologist") An individual who runs lights, sound, or other specialized equipment.

Theatre-in-the-round (see **Arena stage**)

Thrust stage A contemporary stage design in which the acting area extends beyond the proscenium into the audience. The audience sits on three sides of this stage.

Tormentor (see **Leg**)

Trap An opening in the stage floor with a removable cover.

Traveler A curtain that extends the full length and height of the stage and can be raised or pulled to reveal a scene or to be used as a *border* or *legs*.

Tread The horizontal board (which has width and depth) in a step or stair unit.

Trim To adjust curtains, electrics, or flown scenery so that they are level or parallel with the floor and/or are properly masked or hidden from view.

Turntable A revolving stage.

Understudy (also called "standby") An actor who is assigned to learn and rehearse a role for which another actor has been cast. The understudy performs only if the person originally cast in the role cannot perform.

Upstage A position or movement away

from the audience (toward the back of the stage), as opposed to down-stage or toward the audience.

Upstaging To step upstage of another actor, causing that actor to turn away from the audience in order to share the scene.

Wagon A platform on casters that may be brought onstage for a quick scene change. The wagon may be part of the new scenery or just a ve-hicle for moving it.

Walk-on A short role with few or no lines.

Walk the curtain To assist or assure the complete closing of the curtain by walking behind it as it is drawn.

Warning A signal from the stage man-ager that a cue is coming soon.

Wings Offstage right and left where actors and crew wait for entrances or work the show.

Work lights Lights used for illumina-tion during rehearsals or technical work sessions.

INDEX